Ashley Tisdale

Life Is Sweet!

An Unauthorized Biography
by Grace Norwich

PRICE STERN SLOAN
Published by the Penguin Group
Penguin Group (USA) Inc., 375 Hudson Street,
New York, New York 10014, U.S.A.
Penguin Group (Canada), 90 Eglinton Avenue East, Suite 700,
Toronto, Ontario, Canada M4P 2Y3
(a division of Pearson Penguin Canada Inc.)
Penguin Books Ltd, 80 Strand, London WC2R 0RL, England
Penguin Ireland, 25 St Stephens Green, Dublin 2, Ireland
(a division of Penguin Books Ltd)
Penguin Group (Australia), 250 Camberwell Road,
Camberwell, Victoria 3124, Australia
(a division of Pearson Australia Group Pty Ltd)
Penguin Books India Pvt Ltd, 11 Community Centre,
Panchsheel Park, New Delhi - 110 017, India
Penguin Group (NZ), Cnr Airborne and Rosedale Roads,
Albany, Auckland 1310, New Zealand
(a division of Pearson New Zealand Ltd)
Penguin Books (South Africa) (Pty) Ltd, 24 Sturdee Avenue,
Rosebank, Johannesburg 2196, South Africa

Penguin Books Ltd, Registered Offices:
80 Strand, London WC2R 0RL, England

Photo credits: Cover: courtesy of Jeffery Mayer/Star File. Insert photos: first page,
third page, and fourth page courtesy of Jeffery Mayer/Star File; second page
courtesy of Walt Disney Television/Photofest © Walt Disney Television. Cover
and insert background courtesy of mayang.com.

Library of Congress Control Number: 2006020967

Special Markets ISBN-13 978-0-8431-2667-9; ISBN-10 0-8431-2667-1
Not for resale

Ashley Tisdale

Life Is Sweet!

An Unauthorized Biography
by Grace Norwich

PSS!
PRICE STERN SLOAN

Contents

Introduction

The Sweet Life of Ashley Tisdale

shley Tisdale is far from just another pretty Hollywood face! A solid triple threat with an amazing vocal range, dance skills, and great acting chops, Ashley is a superstar in the making. But this beautiful and talented star of the hit Disney Channel show *The Suite Life of Zack & Cody* and the phenomenally successful Disney Channel movie *High School Musical* has her head on straight. While other stars her age are out club-hopping and gunning for spots in *Us Weekly* and *OK!*, Ashley can be found hanging out in her condo with her mom and her puppy. But don't let her laid-back demeanor fool you. Ashley is one powerhouse of a performer who can morph from character to character without batting an eyelash. It's been a long road, but even though she's living the sweet life now, Ashley is still the girl-next-door from New Jersey that she was when she started out.

Chapter 1
Fun Fast Facts

You're Ashley's number-one fan. You never miss an episode of *The Suite Life* and you've seen *High School Musical* a thousand times. You don't even need the DVD sing-along version to belt out the musical numbers. And now you're reading this book. So you think you know everything there is to know about Ashley? Well, check out these essential biographical details to make sure that you have your Ashley Tisdale facts straight.

1. Name: Ashley Michelle Tisdale

2. Birthday: July 2, 1985

3. Birthplace: West Deal, New Jersey

4. Height: 5 feet 3 inches

5. Eyes: Brown

6. Current home: Valencia, California

7. Zodiac sign: Cancer

8. Parents: Lisa and Mike Tisdale

9. Siblings: Older sis, Jennifer Tisdale (also an actress and her closest friend)

10. Famous relatives: Grandfather Arnold Morris, who made Ginsu knives popular, and cousin Ron Popeil, an inventor

11. Favorite color: Pink

12. Favorite food: Sushi, but absolutely no eel—ever!

13. Food she can't live without: Peanut Butter Cap'n Crunch and vanilla ice blend from Coffee Bean. Ashley can't start her morning without either.

14. Her hidden talent: She loves to go horseback riding!

15. The name of Ashley's pet Maltipoo puppy:
    Blondie—it actually comes from Ashley's
    own nickname on *The Suite Life*.

16. Favorite books: *The Great Gatsby,* by F. Scott
    Fitzgerald. Ashley loves to read and sneaks
    little moments on set to dig into a good book.
    Sometimes she indulges in more fun fiction, like
    the series *The A-List,* by Zoey Dean. "It's kind of
    like *Laguna Beach* set in a book in Beverly Hills,"
    she told teenhollywood.com. That's right up
    Ashley's alley.

17. Favorite music: Ashley loves Billy Joel as a solo
    artist, but her new favorite band is The Used.

18. Favorite car: A silver Range Rover

19. Favorite movie: *Peter Pan,* with Jeremy
    Sumpter. She's crazy for Tinkerbell (when she
    isn't watching chick flicks about weddings, or
    Laguna Beach on TV).

20. Favorite actors: Brittany Murphy, Julia Roberts, Johnny Depp, and Leonardo DiCaprio

21. Why Ashley loves acting: She can shed her image and become whomever she wants to be, as she told her official website, ashleytisdale.com: "I get to be different characters that tell different stories."

Chapter 2

Down-to-Earth Star

Ashley Tisdale has become a world-class celebrity by playing the girl you love to hate, Sharpay Evans, in the mega-hit Disney movie *High School Musical*. But in reality, the young actress is one of the sweetest stars you could ever know.

Sure, she's beautiful and blond, with a closet full of amazing clothes (well, maybe more like three or four closets). She is so famous that people ask for her autograph wherever she goes, and sometimes groups of kids chant her name when she hits hot rock concerts. She has producers and directors knocking down her door to read their scripts, and she makes plenty of money.

But Ashley doesn't let any of that go to her head. Despite all the glitz and glamour of her everyday existence, which has been made increasingly complicated with her rising stardom, she relishes the simple things in life, like hanging out with friends, doing creative things, shopping, and just flashing that big smile of hers when she launches into one of her favorite activities: laughing.

"I'm really nice and sweet. If you see me, you can totally come up to me. I'll totally say hi," Ashley said in 2005 to thestarscoop.com. "I'm really funny. I try to make people laugh. I love to make people laugh. It's, like, such a cool thing in the world to have people smile and laugh at me."

Yeah, that's right. Ashley will do pretty much anything for a laugh, and she isn't too famous to laugh at herself.

Ashley gets her humility from the fact that she hasn't always been a star. She understands what it means to be quiet, far from the center of attention. Even though now she's a successful actress, Ashley was actually really timid and reserved when she was a young kid. She was anything but the class clown while growing up in suburban New Jersey.

But there was a spark in Ashley, that something special, as they say in the business. Her acting talents and great face for the small screen were discovered soon enough. Ashley launched a career and moved to California with her family to be closer to the action. Although now she has relocated to the land of convertibles and skim double lattes, appeared on television and on magazine covers, and gained millions of adoring fans, Ashley has never forgotten her roots. She has even worked at a store at the mall, just like any normal teen!

Because she's super-close with her family, her parents and big sister, Jennifer, are always on hand to put her in her place if she ever gets too high on herself. Not that she needs it, since she's so down to earth. They are there for good stuff as well, like offering a shoulder (or shoulders) to cry on if she doesn't get a part. As the baby of the family, Ashley still relies on her family a lot. When she flies, she gets so nervous that she has to have her mom and her stuffed animal with her.

A celebrity who travels with her mom and a stuffed animal? Ashley definitely gives off a wholesome image, and she's not ashamed of that. In fact, that's exactly what she wants to portray. She's a different kind of star from the typical young actress or musician who gives off a bad-girl image, wearing seductive outfits, writhing around on videos, and freaking out at public events. Ashley rebels against this mode of celebrity. She loves clothes just as much as the next celebrity, but you'll never see her in boy shorts, belly-baring shirts, and stilettos. No stomach or tongue piercing for this ingénue. Ashley dresses modestly. Her style is tasteful but supercool. Her long, glossy blond hair, designer duds, and winning smile even attracted the sophisticated *New York Times* Style section, which singled her out for a fantastic wardrobe that suits her age. Modesty certainly works for Ashley. Lots of girls aspire to be like her, and luckily she's someone worthy of role-model status.

When Ashley auditioned for the Disney Channel's *The Suite Life of Zack & Cody,* a sitcom about twin boys who live in a hotel, she actually tried out for the part of the spoiled and snobby hotel owner's daughter, London Tipton. She also auditioned to play the role of the lovable babysitter and candy-counter clerk, Maddie Fitzpatrick, which of course eventually became the part that would make her famous. It's not just pure fate or luck that Ashley hit it big playing the character of Maddie, who is as sweet as the treats she sells. No, Ashley was totally psyched that she landed the part of a positive, happy character over a mean teen because it fit with her true personality. Maddie's sunny disposition was something she could totally relate to, and you know what they say about acting, writing, or art: Start with what you know.

That gave Ashley a great base to work from and allowed her to go on to roles that would challenge her range of acting, like that of Sharpay. But even though in *High School*

Musical she plays someone with a lot of attitude, it's still a Disney production, just like *The Suite Life of Zack & Cody*. And Disney is a company Ashley definitely feels really secure and content working for. Just take a look at the example of *High School Musical* alone. While the musical phenomenon has been compared to huge hits of the past, such as *Grease* or *Dirty Dancing*, the Disney movie differs in that it doesn't have any sex, drugs, bad language, and, oh yeah, cigarettes.

A lot of people think that *High School Musical*'s old-fashioned take on teens is the reason it has become a pop culture sensation. Even though celebrities like Britney Spears, Christina Aguilera, and Jessica Simpson made names for themselves by acting sexy at an early age, a lot of kids just want to be, well, kids. "There's only one kiss in the film, and it's on the cheek. Its success contradicts the perception people have of kids being jaded, oversexualized, and more sophisticated than their age," explained children's marketing expert Chris Byrne to the *Chicago Sun-Times* in 2006. "It speaks to the inherent innocence of children."

Let's face it, you can't get much more innocent than the company that gave birth to Mickey Mouse. Ashley says that Disney is a perfect match for her age and her artistic sensibility.

"I love Disney because I'm really, really young still. I never really felt comfortable, even before I was on Disney, doing any type of roles that are really mature," she said in an interview to thestarscoop.com. "I always want to work for Disney my whole life. It keeps you with such a safe feeling that, you know, you don't have to show skin or do any of that stuff. It's comfortable, and I love the characters I portray. I figure this is where I want to be right now. I don't want to do all those mature roles right now. I have my whole life to do that."

So Ashley is an old-fashioned star, or maybe a new breed of star. The point is, she's a great girl. She's best buds with her folks, looks out for her costars, appreciates her fans, and understands that she needs to give it her all if she wants to stay on top in her demanding career. But maybe the best thing about Ashley is that she believes in dreams, not just for herself but for everyone else, too. Just like the message offered in *High School Musical*, Ashley believes fantasies can come true. "Always follow your dreams!" she told KriSeLen.com. "But remember you have to work hard. You can't expect it to be given to you. But never give up because you can do anything you want."

Chapter 3

Jersey Girl

Ashley Tisdale was born on July 2, 1985, in Monmouth County, New Jersey. Her parents, Lisa and Mike, glowed with pride when they brought their beautiful, brown-eyed girl home from the hospital to the family house in the town of West Deal. This is a typical all-American community, with lots of tree-lined streets, pretty parks, and freshwater lakes, with the Atlantic Ocean not too far away. It's also just a couple of hours' drive from New York City and the bright lights of Broadway, where Ashley would one day see her name lit up. But all that would have to wait.

Ashley's younger years were about as normal as they come. Her parents were definitely the doting types, showering lots of love and affection on Ashley and her older sister, Jennifer, who would also go on to be an actress. Obviously the two girls were used to getting a lot of attention from an early age, or they wouldn't be so comfortable performing onstage and in front of the camera as young women.

Actually, fame and celebrity are sort of in Ashley's blood. Her grandfather on her mother's side, Arnold Morris, is famous for developing Ginsu knives. In case you aren't a big cook, these are the supersharp knives that used to be advertised all the time on late-night "infomercials." These hammy commercials featured chefs in big hats using the knives to do all sorts of unbelievable things, like cutting tin cans in half and slicing rubber auto parts. (Okay, so none of that's as cool as starring in a Broadway musical and in a hit show on the Disney Channel, but still, Grandpa was pretty well-known in his time—just ask your own grandparents!)

Ashley is also related to another "famous" inventor named Ronald Popeil, though his inventions are even wackier than the Ginsu knives that cut through anything. For instance, maybe you've heard of a nifty little contraption called the Veg-O-Matic food slicer? Or the Popeil Pocket Fisherman? Or the Inside-the-Shell Egg Scrambler? No? Well, believe it or not, they're all the brainchildren of one of Ashley's distant relatives.

Growing up in New Jersey, Ashley did a lot of the same things kids in towns across America do. That included spending tons of time with her parents and her older and equally cute sister Jennifer. In fact, on the official Ashley Tisdale website, ashleytisdale.com, the star doesn't have to think for a second about what her one true favorite thing in the world is: "My family!" she declared. In another interview, this time with the *Miami Herald,* in 2005, Ashley was asked who was the most influential person in her life. She replied, "My mom. She has helped me get where I am today. She is my support and my best friend. I love her."

While the Tisdale parents must have sensed that Ashley (and her sister, too) had plenty of star potential, they were careful about instilling really positive values in their children. Growing up, the Tisdale girls definitely had none of the pampering that the characters Zack and Cody are used to on *The Suite Life*. Just the opposite. "I always had a normal life," Ashley explained to *American Cheerleader* in February 2006. "I worked at Wet Seal in the mall and went to a regular school. My dad wanted me to know how long it took to make money and not to take anything for granted." (If you're wondering, Wet Seal is a store that sells women's casual sportswear, which might explain where Ashley got her rockin' fashion sense.)

School was always a priority in the Tisdale household. Though Ashley no doubt spent a lot of hours hanging out with friends and shopping at the nearby mall (when she didn't have to work there, that is), the fun activities would have only been allowed after her homework was done. "My dad is adamant about education," Ashley told celeb101.com. "My sister graduated from college, and I cut a deal with him. He agreed to let me film some pilots as long as I took as many classes in music and acting as I could."

It was obvious from an early age that Ashley was blessed with loads of musical talent. Besides having an amazing voice, she also proved to be pretty good with instruments. "I have a really good ear with music," she said during an interview with *Scholastic News* online. "I can play piano by ear, which means I can listen to a song and play it on the piano. Melodies just kind of come up in my head. I have a voice teacher who showed me how [to write] lyrics." (Listen up, any of you aspiring performers who dread going to piano lessons each week. Lessons definitely helped turn Ashley into the mega-huge star she is today!)

Despite these natural musical abilities and her gift for

acting that Ashley is so well-known for today, she was actually more studious than you might expect. You can just as easily picture her with her nose buried in a book in school as you can imagine her belting out show tunes on stage. "My favorite subject was English or creative writing," she confirmed on ashleytisdale.com. "We did poems and made a magazine and I did one on celebrities. I called it *Celebrity Life* magazine." Obviously she had plenty of smarts *and* a desire to be famous.

Ashley was also a lot more reserved than most of the characters she went on to play on television. "When I was in school I was friendly with everybody," she told *Scholastic News* online, describing the difference between herself and Sharpay, the often mean-spirited character she played in *High School Musical*. "Believe it or not I was kind of quiet—I get that from my dad. My mom is really outgoing."

In addition to being a little on the shy side, it sounds like Ashley could be a bit of a klutz, as well. Talking to teenhollywood.com about one of her embarrassing moments, Ashley shares this story: "I was in school and I was running in P.E.—two miles! We were running on the sidewalk and I saw some cute guy on the other side of the street and I ran into a fire hydrant and flipped over it and landed on the sidewalk and the sprinklers were on, so I got soaked." Talk about doing flips for a boy!

So what happened? How did Ashley turn from this shy kid who used to run into things to a suave, sophisticated superstar with millions of adoring fans? Well, the loving parents and supportive home life were definitely a huge part of it. But she also credits one of America's oldest pastimes with making her more outgoing: cheerleading. "My sister was a hard-core cheerleader, and I always wanted to follow her," Ashley said in an interview with *American Cheerleader*. "I was really shy when I was younger, and cheerleading helped me come out of my shell."

Ashley was about eight years old the first time she put on her own cheerleader uniform. Something about getting up in front of hundreds of fans and rallying their support with nothing more than a smile and a pair of pom-poms unleashed the spirit of performance in her. But as we'll see in the next chapter, the performer in Ashley had already been there for some time. She just needed a good, loud cheer to bring it to life.

Chapter 4
Catching a Star ... in the Mall

It's pretty easy to imagine the scene that day at the Monmouth Mall in Eatontown, New Jersey, back in 1988. The place was no doubt bustling with shoppers, many of them local teenagers wearing neon stockings and the black rubber bracelets that were all the rage in the '80s. But the atmosphere was probably even a little crazier than normal on this particular afternoon, because Bill Perlman, owner of New Talent Management, was conducting a talent search—and he'd chosen the Monmouth Mall as the venue.

Just picture all the young guys and gals lined up, waiting for their audition with the judges. Remember, this was before the days of *American Idol* (or even the Internet), so the feeling must have been that this was their one big shot at stardom.

One person who did not seem very fazed by all the excitement was Ashley Tisdale. But then, she was just a three-year-old being pushed in a stroller through the corridors of the mall by her mother, Lisa. Still, even if Ashley and her mom may not have noticed the event Perlman was putting on, Perlman definitely noticed them. "She had a head full of beautiful curly hair, huge eyes, and when she looked at me, she made the hugest of smiles," Perlman recalled in an interview for the *Asbury Park Press* in 2006. "I followed her into the store and asked if they were going to be participating in the talent show. I was told, 'Not interested, but thanks.' I left them to their shopping knowing with certainty that she had no idea what I could do for them or what she was missing."

Successful talent agents don't get very far in this world by letting a sure thing get away, and Perlman was no different. So when he saw Ashley and her mom later that same day in the mall, he slipped her mom a business card, just on the off chance that she should happen to change her mind. A month or so later, Ashley's mom got in touch with Perlman. Not long after that, Ashley was going on her first audition. True to Perlman's predictions, she nailed it, and landed her first job modeling clothes for JCPenney. Even at three years old, Ashley was already ahead of the trends—it's no wonder she's so stylin' now! Though according to Perlman, Ashley's success goes beyond a big smile and flair for fashion. As he told the *Asbury*

Park Press, "The rest [of Ashley's success] has been lots of good fortune and plenty of work, preparation, and planning."

On the strength of her solid performance in the JCPenney spot, Ashley's commercial career took off and she went on to appear in over one hundred ads nationwide. There are too many to recall, but one in particular stands out from the rest, as much for Ashley's costar as for the product they were selling. That's the T-Mobile television commercial she made with Catherine Zeta-Jones, the gorgeous A-list actress who has been in such films as *The Mask of Zorro*, *Oceans Twelve,* and *Chicago*. She's also married to the equally famous actor, Michael Douglas. Ashley was pretty impressed by Zeta-Jones. When KriSeLen.com asked Ashley about her fondest memory from her commercial, she said, "It was the best experience. For four days I went to Canada and got to work with Catherine Zeta-Jones! She's so nice. It was so much fun!" Apparently, Zeta-Jones took quite a shine to her young bubbly counterpart as well. "At the time, I had curly hair and she'd compliment me on it," Ashley told *People* magazine.

That comment might surprise Ashley's fans, who are used to the pin-straight golden tresses she wears for most of her acting roles and in so many of the photo shoots she does.

But as her personal and professional stylist, Ozlem Dalgic, told *Sophisticate's Hairstyle*: "Ashley naturally has very thick, coarse, curly hair." So you see, just because you were born with one head of hair doesn't mean you can't play around with different dos.

Despite all the success Ashley was having with her acting career, she was the same regular girl at home in New Jersey. Her routine still consisted of the same things: schoolwork, piano lessons, and cheerleading during the week; hanging out with friends and maybe doing a little bit of shopping on the weekends. Her peers and teachers definitely weren't treating her like she was special.

In fact, though Tisdale was now working pretty steadily as a professional actor, she still wasn't landing many plum roles at school. "I didn't get along too well with the drama teachers," Ashley told the *Asbury Park Press* in 2006. "They never wanted to cast me in any parts." But even Ashley admits that the situation was a little tense with her teachers, given that she was often busy (and away from school) attending big city auditions. "I think they didn't like me going on the auditions, so I never got selected for the plays."

If Ashley was bothered about being passed over by the

drama teachers at school, she definitely forgot all about it when, at the age of eight, she was awarded the dream role of Cosette in *Les Misérables* on Broadway. This musical, by Alain Boublil and Claude-Michel Schönberg, with lyrics by Herbert Kretzmer, is one of the most popular and long-running musicals of all time. Opening in London in 1985, *Les Mis*, as it's known, tells the story of a man who is sent to prison for stealing a loaf of bread so that he can feed his family. When the play made it to Broadway two years later, it won eight Tony Awards, including Best Musical. Cosette is a featured part, that of the man's adopted young daughter.

Everything came together smoothly for Ashley when she went out for the role of Cosette. Although singing professionally posed a big challenge, it would launch an entire new side of her career. "Lacey Chabert had been starring in it, and she is one of my really good friends," Ashley told *Scholastic News* online. "She is older than I am and I looked up to her, and I thought she was really cool. I told my manager and he got me an audition for the national tour. My mom threw me into some voice lessons to get me prepared for it. It was a really great experience, and so I have sung ever since then. I love to sing."

Ashley enjoyed playing the part of Cosette so much that she stuck with it from 1993 to 1995. "It was amazing," she told KriSeLen.com. "I think it helped me get to the place where I am today." Not only did she have to memorize lines and learn to sing for a Broadway audience, she also had to perform every day (sometimes even twice a day if there was a matinee) for two years. It took so much energy to perform so often that she didn't have the strength to get nervous. Well, at least after a while. About being in *Les Misérables*, she said, "It taught me discipline and helped me get over being shy. I love doing comedy because it reminds me of theater; you get to perform in front of a live audience."

Performing in front of a live audience would prove to be an invaluable experience to Ashley down the line when she would go on to do television, where actors not only tape in front of a live audience, they also have to work day in and day out like professionals do on Broadway. And getting over her stage jitters only helped Ashley with her confidence when she went to auditions for commercials and TV appearances. Right after her stint in *Les Misérables*, Ashley landed another seminal American play: *Annie*. The original musical—based on an old-fashioned popular comic strip by Harold Gray, called *Little Orphan Annie*—first opened on Broadway at the Alvin Theatre on April 21, 1977, and ran for 2,377 performances! With music by Charles Strouse, lyrics by Martin Charnin, and dialogue by Thomas Meehan, the show, about ten-year-old Annie, who lives in an orphanage in Depression-era New York City, was a massive hit. Audiences fell in love with the little girl with the head of red curls. Every girl wanted to sing and act just like Andrea McArdle, the actress who played the original Annie. The success of the show was reflected in all the professional acclaim it received. *Annie* was nominated for eleven Tony Awards and won seven, including Best Musical. It went on to become a staple of school drama departments across the country, and many famous child actors such as Sarah Jessica Parker and Allison Smith took the role of Annie on Broadway. So Ashley became part of a grand history when she joined the cast of the international touring company of the much-beloved musical and went to places all over the world singing its iconic songs such as "It's the Hard-Knock Life" and "Tomorrow."

As exciting as traveling across the globe sounds, her experience with Broadway musicals also enabled her to visit the one place every kid (and a lot of grown-ups) dream about seeing up close: the White House. It was when Bill Clinton was president and Ashley was part of a troupe of young stage actors. "I was part of [The] Broadway Kids, which was a bunch of kids who were in Broadway shows, and we sang Broadway tunes and met the president," Ashley told *Newsday*. "I was so nervous, but it was really fun." From the mall in New Jersey to the White House in Washington, D.C.—all before Ashley was old enough to go to the prom. Not bad!

Around the same time as her White House performance, Ashley set her sights on another American institution: Hollywood. As much as she loved acting onstage, she no doubt aspired to get on the big screen as well. In 2001, she got an enormous break, appearing in *Donnie Darko*, a strange black comedy starring heartthrob Jake Gyllenhaal. During the filming of the movie, which would go on to become a cult classic, Ashley obviously came to understand why Jake has so many admirers. When teenhollywood.com asked Ashley who her biggest celebrity crush was, she answered, "I'd have to say Jake Gyllenhaal. I worked with him in *Donnie Darko,* so that was really cool." She gave a little bit of an embarrassed laugh during the interview that showed just how much she really meant it! So, Jake, if you're reading this . . .

Actually, at that time, the last thing Ashley had time for was a serious boyfriend, since her television career was really starting to take off.

Chapter 5

Résumé Building

By the time Ashley was a young teen, she had already proven herself to be a versatile actress who could work in a lot of different mediums. She snagged a hundred lucrative commercials. While the pay for those ads was great, she really hoped to make it doing something a little more creative, something that would really entertain people and not just sell cell phones. There was the theater. Singing and dancing were certainly not obstacles for Ashley. And she didn't lose it in front of a live audience of hundreds. And there was film. She'd had a taste of making movies with the cult classic *Donnie Darko* and a small voice role in the much-loved animated flick *A Bug's Life*. Film might be glamorous and the theater is certainly dramatic, but for Ashley, her true love was television.

Ashley's passion for the small screen began at a very young age, and she has stayed true to it for her entire career.

When a reporter from the *Miami Herald* asked Ashley in 2005 which the actress preferred, being on TV or onstage, she didn't skip a beat: "Actually, I prefer TV—even though I love theater, TV is just the best," Ashley said. "I love being on a sitcom and working in front of a live audience. I guess it's kind of like theater in that way, with an audience present, but I still absolutely love TV."

TV is tough. When you plop down on the couch to watch your favorite program, you probably have no idea of the blood, sweat, and tears that went into making it (that's a good thing, since you wouldn't be able to relax and enjoy it if you did). Television is one of the most demanding forms of popular culture. No one would say rock stars who tour all over the country, or people in the theater who go onstage night after night, don't work hard. But when compared to film, television is viewed as the grittiest, most tumultuous, generally most demanding job. Hours on a film set can be torturously long— we're talking eighteen hours a day long—but generally a movie only takes a couple of months for an actor to make. There are exceptions, but often a movie star spends a few exhausting weeks working and then returns to lounge poolside or look for the next part.

For an entire season, a television actor on a series works day in and day out, just like a person with an office job. It can take a whole week to shoot only one episode of a drama. For sitcoms, writers are often changing lines up to the last moment and even during the live-audience taping if they notice that a joke doesn't get a laugh. That requires a lot of flexibility from those who have to deliver the lines. TV actors are rewarded with about three months off during the summer. But a lot of them choose to return to work during that time, either doing plays to hone their thespian skills or auditioning for film roles in order to break into the movies (with those TV schedules, who can blame them for wanting to get into film?).

If you are on a hit show, it's still a lot of work, but it can be the greatest job in show business. That's because it is also very stable work. For a profession as volatile as acting, that means a ton. Also, people who go into acting know that part of the deal is auditioning, auditioning, auditioning, which can get really tiring. Nobody likes to be rejected, even those who are used to it.

But successful shows that run for years and years and years—such as *Friends* or *Charmed*—are one in a million. More often than not, programs are yanked before they've even had a chance to gain a loyal audience if they've gotten bad ratings during their initial episodes. It isn't uncommon to see billboards and signs across buses advertising a show that has been taken off the air so fast that the network didn't have time to stop its commercial campaign.

A lot of shows don't even make it on the air in the first place. There's a whole long process that goes into making the lineup you see on your favorite TV channel during prime time. It starts with writers and producers pitching show ideas to network executives, who usually make up their minds whether they like it or not in about sixty seconds. If the execs give the go-ahead, then the network commissions a pilot, which is a sample of the program that usually sets up the plot and relationships of the characters, which will hopefully have a chance to come alive. The networks order a bunch of these pilots, way more than would ever be able to make it on the air. Then they watch them and decide whether to order more episodes. It's a stomach-churning, nail-biting process for the producers who cook up the ideas and the actors who star in them. Ashley has had her share of disappointments when it comes to pilots. She made two that never got off the ground. One was a comedy for ABC called *The Mayor of Oyster Bay*, which was about a guy with a big ego and big dreams who becomes the mayor of a small city. Ashley also had a part in an untitled NBC pilot with Howie Mandel, the zany Canadian comedian who is famous for not liking to shake people's hands and who recently hit it big as host of the game show *Deal or No Deal*.

Ashley was certainly disappointed that neither of those pilots saw the light of day, or the light of the boob tube. But there's always more than one way to achieve a dream. In 1997, when she was only twelve years old, Ashley made her first guest appearance on a television show. She appeared on *Smart Guy*— a WB show about a genius ten-year-old tenth-grader who has problems fitting in. Ashley played a young girl named Amy in the episode that aired April 30, "A Little Knowledge," where the young genius gets into trouble when he competes on a game show called *Knowledge College*. It was only a tiny part, but it was a start.

Only six months later, her second guest appearance aired. This time it was on another WB program, the long-running classic family drama *7th Heaven,* about a reverend and his wife and all their issues raising seven children with Christian values. Ashley had the part of Janice in the episode

"Breaking Up Is Hard to Do." Landing a part on a show about the trials and tribulations of a pastor's family and friends definitely fit with Ashley's good-girl image. And to get on a show as successful as *7th Heaven* is something that any actor would kill for, since it can only help future casting directors take interest. So it seemed that Ashley's career was off and running.

Not so fast. Even the top stars have a hard time finding work in such a fickle business. Ashley was only a kid from New Jersey, just starting out. She had to continue to go on audition after audition (not to mention keep up with her schoolwork). It wasn't going to come easy. In fact, it would be a whole three years before she would land her next slew of guest appearances.

In the beginning of 2000, Ashley got a part on the iconic '90s teen drama *Beverly Hills 90210*. She played Nicole Loomis in the episode "Fertile Ground." The show was definitely winding down from its heyday when those notorious kids—Kelly, Donna, Dylan, David, Steve, Andrea, Brandon, and Brenda—and their bad behavior in limos and mansions occupied the imagination of practically every teenager in the country. Still, it was a great gig for Ashley to get. There would be plenty more that year, with appearances on *Boston Public,* *The Geena Davis Show,* and *Movie Stars*.

The parts kept on coming for Ashley. She played a runaway teen on the hit supernatural show *Charmed,* with Alyssa Milano, about three sisters who practice witchcraft. She also appeared on such popular shows as *Once and Again* and *Strong Medicine*.

Ashley was cast in shows that ran the gamut of styles and networks, from big casts to small ensembles. But Ashley was starting to get a taste for comedy by appearing on some of TV's funniest shows. The sitcom was a genre for which she would soon show a real talent. In 2002, she had a small role in the hilarious Fox comedy *Malcolm in the Middle,* about a high-school kid played by Frankie Muniz and all the trouble he gets into with his brothers. And she had another minor appearance on another funny Fox show, *Grounded for Life,* starring Donal Logue, Megyn Price, and Kevin Corrigan. She did repeat performances on *The Hughleys*, a UPN comedy about a family that moves from the inner city to the suburbs, and on *George Lopez*, the ABC family show starring the popular standup comedian.

But in 2001, Ashley finally had her goal within grasp

when she landed a regular role on a series. She was all set to play the part of Stephanie on a new Fox sitcom called *Nathan's Choice*. But this wasn't any ordinary television comedy. *Nathan's Choice*—starring J. D. Walsh and cowritten by Chuck Lorre, the cocreator and executive producer behind the popular sitcom *Dharma & Greg*—was going to be a completely interactive show where viewers decided how the plot would unfold. Sounds nuts, right? But a lot of people in the media industry were excited about this experiment. The comedy followed the life of Nathan, a recent college graduate who was totally not ready for real life. While he got into jams, viewers could use their computers or telephones to vote for one of two already-made-up story lines halfway through any given episode. (The "losing" half of the story line was supposed to run on the Fox-owned cable network FX at a later date.)

"The underlying message is that it's not always the big choices you make, but the little ones that can have unbelievable results," Lorre told *Entertainment Weekly* online in 2001, around the time of the pilot. "This is about a naïve young man who can make a lot of bad choices—and the audience is going to help him." Cool concept. But unfortunately it didn't get very far. Network executives killed *Nathan's Choice*. T. S.

Kelly, a Nielsen/NetRatings media analyst, panned the show, telling *Entertainment Weekly* online, "It's still more gimmick than substance. It'll be a test to see if content of this nature will survive." Even Lorre knew it would be hard to make into a success. "It'll be cool if it works," he said. "But it's really complicated. There's no precedent for this."

So, after seven years of acting in television, Ashley proved to be a serious small-screen veteran with twenty-one guest appearances on sixteen programs, two failed pilots, and one regular series that never got off the ground. That was quite an impressive résumé, but this hardworking actress still hadn't achieved her dream: to have a starring role on a successful television show. Many people might have given up, discouraged that despite so many opportunities, none had turned out to be the big jackpot. But, hey, this is Ashley we're talking about. There's no way she would give up on her dream so easily. And it's a good thing she didn't pack it in and return to the East Coast, because her big break was right around the corner.

Chapter 6

Too Suite for Words

$\mathcal{A}$round the time Ashley was starting to wonder if her big break would ever come, the business executives at the Disney Channel—the cable network that airs live-action and animated programs aimed at younger audiences—were also looking for a hit. Not that they were strangers to success. After all, this is the station that created sensations like *Lizzie McGuire*, a popular sitcom running since 2001. But the world of television is a lot of "what have you done for me lately?"—so the executives were growing a little restless.

That's when a couple of television creators named Danny Kallis and Jim Geoghan came to them with an idea for a new live-action comedy. Their working title was *The Suite Life of Zack & Cody*. You never know what shows are going to strike a chord with audiences, so pitch meetings (that's where creative types present their ideas to the "suits" or executives) can often be fraught with suspense. Just imagine trying to sell a bunch of serious, sober businessmen and businesswomen on a show about the lives of crazy kids.

The pitch meeting for *The Suite Life of Zack & Cody* must have been a little weird because the show is about twelve-year-old twins Zack and Cody, who have just moved into a fancy hotel in Boston, Massachusetts, with their single mother, Carey, a big-time singer hired to entertain the hotel guests. As part of Carey's contract, she and her sons have been given a suite to live in on one of the hotel's upper floors. If the hotel manager, Mr. Moseby, expected Zack and Cody to behave like good little boys, was he ever mistaken. Instead, the twins turn the hotel into their own private amusement park, taking full advantage of the swimming pool, game room, and other hotel services. The result is a less than relaxing stay for many of the hotel's guests. The twins also make friends with members of the hotel staff, including Maddie, the candy-counter clerk and their sometimes babysitter.

Though the show promised plenty of hysterical hijinks, it also offered an opportunity to touch on some of the serious issues that affect children today, including divorce and moving homes. It also highlights what happens when kids end up living in a world that includes a lot of room service. That's probably why the Disney executives went for *The Suite Life*. "It gives you back of the house/front of the house," Danny Kallis, one of the show's cocreators, told the *New York Times*. "It gives you blue-collar/white-collar. It gives you the high life, when you can't really afford it."

Once Disney gave *The Suite Life* the green light, it was time to think about assembling the crew. They brought in two talented veteran directors named Henry Chan and Richard Correll. Then the casting agents got down to filling the various parts. The lead roles of Zack and Cody were practically written for real-life twin sensations Cole and Dylan Sprouse—but more on them later.

Casting the supporting parts proved a little trickier. That's often the case with television and movies because creators will often have a certain actor in mind for the lead role when they are writing a script, so they really tailor it to his or her particular strengths. The supporting parts are usually not very clearly defined, so it is harder to find the perfect actors for them. The upside to this is that it allows the actor who gets the part to really own the character and make it his or her own.

Casting agents will pore through hundreds of "head shots" (pictures of actors, along with biographical data and work history), looking for actors who might be right for the part. It can be a pretty random process, actually. Fortunately, because Ashley had worked so hard, appearing in over a hundred commercials and taking small parts here and there in other television shows and even a few movies, her face was familiar to a lot of agents. At some point, the *Suite Life* producers decided to call her in for an audition, though for what part exactly, they couldn't say. "I did a couple of pilots for a network series and finally went for a Disney pilot," Ashley told thestarscoop.com. "I went in and actually tested for both roles, London and Maddie."

Now that audiences know Ashley as the sweet-natured and sensible candy-counter clerk, Maddie, it's almost impossible to imagine her playing London, the spoiled and self-centered daughter of the hotel owner. But the casting agents obviously saw in Ashley a versatile actress who could play either part (and, given the next big role she would land in *High School Musical*, can you fault them?). In the end, though, good triumphed over evil and Ashley was awarded the part of Maddie—much to her relief, as it turned out.

Ashley wanted the audience to love her before they would love to hate her, as they would when she played Sharpay in *High School Musical*. "I'm really glad that I ended up with Maddie, because for fans to first get to know me, I'd rather them look up to this character who is more like me, rather than Sharpay," she told thestarscoop.com. Brenda Song, the beautiful actress who got the role of snooty London Tipton, had already been on Disney for a long time, so Ashley explained, "It's easier to see that she's not like that."

The part was right, the setting was right, and even the network was right. In fact, Ashley was absolutely thrilled to be acting on the Disney Channel. The channel is known as a family network, which refers mainly to the type of wholesome shows it airs (no violence or foul language there, thank you very much). But it also describes the community of actors it has fostered over the years. In a way, being on a show that airs on the Disney Channel is like being initiated into an exclusive club. Think of all the super-talented stars who got their start at Disney—from Britney Spears to Justin Timberlake to Hilary Duff, and more.

Ashley also didn't have to worry about not knowing anyone when she showed up at the Disney studios. She was already friends with Raven-Symone Pearman, the star of the Disney show *That's So Raven*, as well as the gorgeous sisters and talented musical duo Alyson Renae "Aly" and Amanda Joy "AJ" Michalka. Aly, a star on the hit Disney series *Phil of the Future*, was also the star of the channel's original movie *Now You See It*. The sisters, who have written and performed music for some of their shows, costar in the Disney TV series *Haversham Hall*.

"It's fate that I ended up there," Ashley said to thestarscoop.com. "I've known Raven since I was three. I hadn't seen her for the longest time! Now I'm in the same hallway as her. It's crazy. I've known Aly and AJ since they were really little. We were in acting class together." And, as if that weren't enough, Ashley had even met her costar Brenda. "I've known Brenda since I did a Bette Midler show," Ashley said. "Once you're in the business, you just kind of get to know everybody. You audition with these people, you're friends with these people. I always stay friends with everybody."

Not that it would be all fun and relaxation. As Ashley had already learned, working in television is a tough life. That's true even if you get to be on a show with a lot of close friends. Even if the executives at the Disney Channel create a nice environment for their actors, they still want their programs to succeed and make money for the company. That translates into plenty of hard work and long hours.Fortunately, Ashley had the experience of her childhood to draw on, in particular the lessons her father had taught her about the meaning of an honest day's labor. With that and all the love both parents had given her, she was confident that she would rise to the challenge of *The Suite Life*. Now, she was just excited to get started.

Chapter 7

Home Away from Home: Life on *The Suite Life*

T he first day on the set of a new show can be a lot like the first day of school. Everybody is usually super-excited but also a little on the nervous side. After all, for every new series that goes on to become a huge, gigantic hit, there are dozens that end up getting panned by the critics and yanked from the lineup. And it's almost impossible to predict the winners from the losers. (Otherwise, do you think the big-shot executives would waste their money making flops!?)

Besides being worried that their show might bomb, actors also fret over whether or not they'll get along with the rest of the cast. The entertainment industry is full of stories of television shows and big-screen movies failing because of a lack of chemistry between their actors.

If Ashley had any of these fears or reservations that first day of shooting *The Suite Life*, she sure didn't show it. In fact, she told *Popstar!* magazine that the first day on set was "exciting and happy." But then, unlike many actors in similar situations, she had plenty to be excited and happy about.

For one thing, she was pretty confident that *The Suite Life* was going to succeed. Her reason? Well, she had two, actually: Their names were Cole and Dylan Sprouse. Television has no shortage of pint-sized superstars (just check out the careers of Mary-Kate and Ashley Olsen), but even with so many accomplished child stars coming before them, there was something extra-special about the Sprouses.

The twins were born fifteen minutes apart (Dylan is older), on August 4, 1992, in Arezzo, Italy. Their parents must have suspected that their boys were bound for fame, since they named them after stars: Cole for the famous jazz singer Nat King Cole, and Dylan after the lionized Irish poet, Dylan Thomas.

After their family returned to Southern California from Europe, the twins waited all of six months before starting their careers in front of the camera. Their first gig was a commercial selling toilet paper! They obviously had star quality, because right away they were tapped to play Brett Butler's youngest child, Patrick Kelly, on the hit ABC series *Grace Under Fire* (like the Olsen twins, they often shared the same part).

The stellar job they did on that show led to other television appearances, including *Friends*, where they played the son of Ross (David Schwimmer).

Though the Sprouses worked steadily throughout most of the '90s, their true breakout moment didn't come until 1999, when they appeared opposite Adam Sandler in the smash-hit movie *Big Daddy*. That's where audiences got their first true taste of the irresistible Sprouses. Among their newest and most ardent admirers was none other than Ashley Tisdale. "When *Big Daddy* came out, I fell in love with the boys and told my mom I was going to work with them someday," Ashley recalled in an interview with *Popstar!* magazine. "When I found out they were in [*The Suite Life*], I freaked out and said, 'I have to get this job!'"

Being able to work with the Sprouses was probably the best thing about Ashley's new job, but it wasn't the only thing. She would also be reunited with one of her closest friends in the industry: Brenda Song, who plays the part of London, the spoiled and sometimes spiteful daughter of the hotel owner. Though Brenda is a few years younger than Ashley (she was born on March 27, 1988), the two actresses are the closest of friends. "Brenda and I are like sisters," Ashley told *American*

Cheerleader magazine. "I knew her for four years before the show even started. It's the coolest thing to get to work with my best friend."

So, between the Sprouse twins and Brenda Song, Ashley was pretty psyched about her new cast mates. But not even she was prepared for how totally sweet life on *The Suite Life* would be. Of course, the days are long, just like they are on the set of any television show. But, like the saying goes: "Time flies when you're having fun"—so it hardly felt like work for Ashley and company. "It's so great," Ashley said to KriSeLen.com. "We all work really hard, but when we have lunch breaks, Brenda and I are always getting our nails done or going shopping. Everyone's a huge family. It's great to get to work with people you love."

The family comparison is repeated by just about everyone involved in the making of *The Suite Life*, and that definitely contributes to its success. As any actor will tell you, the best shows are the ones where the cast gets along well and genuinely enjoys coming to work. And it doesn't hurt having a couple of pranksters like Cody and Dylan on hand to provide occasional comic relief. "They're so funny and normal, like boys," Ashley said on mediavillage.com. "They play nonstop.

They just don't care. That's the best part about them." Despite their flair for hijinks, the Sprouses are also respectful of their coworkers, which Ashley attributes to positive upbringing (something else she can relate to). "Their dad has really kept them grounded," she told mediavillage.com. "When they're off from work they're hanging out with their friends and not doing events and stuff. That's really refreshing."

The Sprouses obviously think highly of their coworkers as well, especially Ashley and Brenda, whom they seem to view almost like big sisters. "They're really, really nice," Cole offered in an article for *Tiger Beat* magazine. "I've met some celebrities that are pretty mean. Ashley and Brenda are just naturally cool." That's high praise coming from a boy.

Even though the Sprouses are quite a bit younger than Ashley, their praise must feel pretty good. After all, they are the stars of *The Suite Life*, which was apparent from day one of the filming (not that the twins ever hold it over people's heads; they really are as humble as they come). The title characters, Zack and Cody, were created specifically with Dylan and Cole in mind. "[The Disney creators] asked us what type of show we would want if we had our own show," explained Dylan to *Popstar!* magazine in 2005. "The writers spent a lot of time getting to know us, so our characters are based on what we're like in real life."

The Zack/Dylan character is more of a mischief-maker. He's not that interested in school, and he would much rather spend the afternoon playing video games and getting up to no good. The Cody/Cole character, on the other hand, is sweet and innocent and a terrific student. He's often the unwitting accomplice to his brother's pranks, getting sucked into the shenanigans without even realizing it.

Though these parts were pretty clearly defined, the supporting cast of characters took some time to flesh out. As we already know, Ashley actually tried out for the parts of Maddie *and* London. She was relieved to get the part of the candy-counter clerk because it's similar to how she is in real life. "She is a lot like me. I love her style. She's a little bit more sarcastic than I am," Ashley said, describing Maddie to *Scholastic News* online. "She's a funny girl and always getting into trouble with London, but she always knows how to get out of it; she's a really smart girl and I love portraying someone who is really smart."

Despite the similarities, it still took Ashley a little while to grow into the part. As with any acting role, hair and makeup was a big help, literally transforming Ashley into Maddie. A new hairdo was part of the reinvention, according to Ozlem Dalgic, one of the show's lead stylists. "We lightened [Ashley's] basic hair color to a light beige-blond and then highlighted throughout," she told *Sophisticate's Hairstyle*. "The character Maddie is very smart, but fun and kind of quirky and spunky! I think her hairstyle suits that character in the fact that it's so textured. It's a very fun cut but, at the same time, it's a very smart cut."

The new coif definitely helped Ashley get into character. From there, it was just a matter of practicing her lines and letting herself become Maddie. Actors have all sorts of tricks that help them prepare for a part. They often draw from real-life experiences. For instance, though Ashley never worked as a candy-counter clerk, she did have a job at the mall when she was growing up. No doubt, the experience of dealing with the occasionally snooty customer gave her some good insights into what it might be like to work in a fancy hotel.

After a few weeks of rehearsal Mondays through Fridays, things really started to click for Ashley and the cast. They often perform in front of a live studio audience, which many actors find energizing (as opposed to just performing for the camera). Ashley, always the cheerleader, is responsible for warming up the crowd. "Every morning on show days I always do the welcome speech," she told *American Cheerleader* magazine. "I do this whole speech with so much energy, and then, at the very end, I do a high kick. When you bring lots of energy to things, everyone just becomes more happy."

Her energy definitely did the trick. The show premiered on March 18, 2005, with the episode titled "Hotel Hangout." In that first show, Zack and Cody make friends with Max and Tapeworm, while Maddie develops a crush on Lance, the hotel lifeguard. The episode had its share of pranks, laughs, and even a few semi-serious moments. It really set the tone for the season, and audiences were almost immediately hooked.

Every show that followed was equally anticipated by the growing legion of fans. Though it's hard for Ashley to single out her one favorite episode, she clearly enjoyed some more than others. "I loved 'Rockstar in the House,' with Jesse McCartney," she said to *Scholastic News* online about working with the pop-star sensation who also happens to be a hottie. "He is so cute. It was such a great episode and so much fun to do. There was so much for me, London, and Zack to do. It was really cool and a great experience working with Jesse."

As *The Suite Life* started to generate a larger and larger following, Ashley got her first taste of true celebrity (and the riches that come with it). She splurged on a new car and clothes, though she's always been careful about not going overboard with the material possessions. She also started to develop a real fan base. At first, it was a little strange to be spotted in public, but Ashley got used to it soon enough. One afternoon she entered a local restaurant and ". . . ten little girls at dinner for a birthday started screaming when I walked in," she said with a smile in an interview for missoandfriends.com.

Ashley also experienced the buzz and excitement of mixing with other stars. "I'm a huge fan of Brittany Murphy," she confided to *American Cheerleader* magazine. "I saw her at the Nickelodeon Kids' Choice Awards and went up to her, not knowing what she'd be like, and she was the nicest person! She talked to me for, like, twenty minutes and told me to never give up on my dreams."

All in all, things were looking pretty good for Ashley. As she said to *Sophisticate's Hairstyle*, "I'm so happy with *The Suite Life*. I just believe this is where I'm supposed to be because I'm the happiest." As happy as Ashley was, it was probably impossible for her to imagine life getting any better.

But something was about to happen that promised to blow everything else out of the water.

Chapter 8

High School Musical: Here We Come!

Musicals are about as American as the Stars and Stripes or apple pie. But they're not always considered the height of cool. How many of your friends have show tunes from *Oklahoma!* or *The Sound of Music* piping through their iPods? Every now and then, though, a musical comes along that really shakes up the genre. In the 1970s there was *Grease*, a coming-of-age saga about a good girl who falls for a bad boy with slicked-back hair and a leather jacket. Then in the 1980s there was *Flashdance*, which told the story of a Philadelphia welder who aspired to be a ballerina. In the 1990s, audiences went wild for *Rent*, the stage sensation that put lyrics to bohemian life in New York City.

But the current generation didn't have its trailblazing musical to gyrate to. Always on the lookout for cultural holes in need of filling, the creative executives at Disney sensed an opportunity. They pulled together some of the most talented people in the industry to whip up a story. We don't have to tell you what the talent came back with. *High School Musical* is without a doubt one of the hugest song-and-dance extravaganzas of the new millennium.

Like most successful creations, the story line to *High School Musical* is pretty simple. The romantic comedy takes place at East High, a fictitious school located in Albuquerque, New Mexico. The action revolves around the unlikely relationship that bubbles up between BMOC (that's big man on campus) Troy Bolton and the shy, studious Gabriella Montez after they perform a duet at a local karaoke contest during the winter vacation. When they realize they attend the same high school, they decide to pursue their passion for singing together and try out for the leads in the musical.

That's where it would have ended happily ever after, except for one small problem: teen drama queen Sharpay Evans. Along with her brother, Ryan, Sharpay has starred in her school's musicals for the past ten years (since kindergarten!) and she's not about to surrender the spotlight to a couple of amateur upstarts. Making matters worse for Troy and Gabriella, Troy's basketball teammates and Gabriella's fellow scholastic decathletes have their own reasons to want the budding courtship to crash and burn. But in the end, love—and music—conquers all, and Troy and Gabriella win the leads in the musical, not to mention each other's hearts and the admiration of their peers.

High School Musical is a classic boy-meets-girl story, and that's probably why it has struck a cord with fans. It is the kind of movie that all audiences can relate to—female and male, young kids and older ones—which was very much the plan all along. "I wanted to make a film that didn't speak down to anyone," the film's producer, Bill Borden, told the Florida Sun-Sentinel. In so doing, he looked to the timeless love stories for inspiration. "I drew from a lot of things. I love Franco Zeffirelli's Romeo and Juliet. That was one of my biggest influences, seeing that when I was a freshman in high school. The whole balcony scene in [High School Musical] was influenced by that."

It may sound strange to hear that High School Musical was influenced by a play written by William Shakespeare, but if you know your Elizabethan theater, you know that the Bard (as Shakespeare was commonly called) was writing for the masses, not just the noble classes. The creative team behind High School Musical also wanted to generate widespread appeal.

Injecting lots of singing and dancing into the script seemed like a surefire way to crank up the energy and enthusiasm.

Given that the action takes place in a high school with hundreds of students, this made for some fairly complicated scenes. So Disney brought an accomplished director-choreographer named Danny Ortega on board to execute the production. He had already directed and choreographed the made-for-Disney movie *Newsies*, so the company executives knew they were getting a reliable professional. But, more importantly, Ortega had quality experience overseeing large dance scenes. For instance, he was the lead choreographer on the wildly popular movie *Dirty Dancing*, which starred Patrick Swayze as a dance instructor at a summer camp retreat. Ortega also choreographed the big-production parade scene from the school-cutting classic *Ferris Bueller's Day Off*, which involved hundreds of extras winding their way through the streets of Chicago. Clearly, this guy had the chops to take on *High School Musical*.

Ortega already had a script to work with, which was written by Peter Barsocchini, whose past credits included *Shadow-Ops* and *Drop Zone*. Barsocchini had delivered a strong story, but what the production really needed was some show-stopping musical numbers. Rather than rely on one songwriter, Ortega and producer Bill Borden decided to assemble several pop songwriting teams. The teams were chosen for their distinctive styles, which explains the wonderful range of sounds in the movie, from cute and catchy to slow and sentimental. The songwriters were also very adept at incorporating exact lines from Barsocchini's script into the lyrics, so the singing scenes and regular speaking ones blend together seamlessly.

With the script in place and the musical numbers just in need of some fine-tuning, the production team was able to turn its attention to finding a place to shoot the movie. After scouting several locations throughout the American Southwest, they settled on Salt Lake City, Utah. It looked enough like Albuquerque, New Mexico (where the action is supposed to take place), plus, Ortega knew the city well from the work he had done there for the 2002 Winter Olympics.

They were ready to go! Well, almost. There was just one final matter: casting the movie. A few hundred miles away, Ashley Tisdale was wrapping up another season of *The Suite Life*, wondering how on earth she was going to spend her twelve-week break from the show.

Chapter 9

Drama Queen

The Suite Life of Zack & Cody, like most shows on television, is shot one season at a time. Let's say there are twenty-five episodes in a season. The actors and crew will spend about six months filming those shows, then take a few months off. Most actors relish their vacation time. But like you already know, Ashley Tisdale isn't like most actors. As a result, she wasn't much looking forward to her time away from the set of The Suite Life.

"I literally went on hiatus for [The] Suite Life last summer," she told thestarscoop.com. "I love working. When I'm not working, I get so bored. I was, like, what am I going to do for, like, a couple of months? I don't know what I'm going to do. So for two weeks on hiatus, I was already bored. I was, like, I need to do something."

Fortunately for Ashley, the casting agents hired for High School Musical were gearing up for their next assignment. They knew they wanted some fresh faces to appear in the movie, so they sent out a casting call that literally anyone could respond to. Hundreds of actors did, so the competition for the main roles was really intense.

But Ashley had one advantage: The movie's producer, Bill Borden, was already familiar with her work. "I didn't know any of these kids except for Ashley Tisdale," he told the *Florida Sun-Sentinel*. "I knew her from the Disney show [*The Suite Life of Zack & Cody*]." Clearly, all the hard work she put in was starting to pay off. But that doesn't mean parts were just being handed to her. She had to prove there was a role right for her in *this* film.

"Suddenly, *High School Musical* came around and I went to audition for it," she said to thestarscoop.com. "It wasn't given to me. A lot of people think it is because I'm on Disney, but I had to go on the audition, and to the callback. It wasn't like it was handed to me at all. I had to go in there and get it myself."

Besides her vast television experience, the fact that Ashley toured with the Broadway musical *Les Misérables* also impressed the production team. They definitely wanted her to be in the movie, but for which part? Given how likable Ashley's character Maddie is on *The Suite Life,* she probably figured she'd be a shoo-in for the part of Gabriella, the brainy Goody Two-shoes. So it must have been a huge surprise when the producers called to tell her that she'd been awarded the role of Sharpay, the popular It girl who rules the school.

What a departure this would be from her character of Maddie! But Ashley wasn't complaining. After all, the more characters an actress plays, the better she becomes at capturing different attitudes and emotions. Ashley really understood this. "[The characters] are totally different," she said on thestarscoop.com. "Maddie's, like, this girl next door, she's really, really smart, she gets along with everybody. She's always doing something crazy or insane. She's really sweet, and Sharpay is just the total opposite. She's the most popular girl, she dresses like she's going to a red-carpet event. It's funny because she's mean, but she always has a smile on. But they're totally different."

To help get into the character of Sharpay, Ashley watched a bunch of films that featured equally mean-spirited characters. "I watched a lot of movies to prepare for playing her," she told mediavillage.com. "I actually watched *Mean Girls*, with Rachel McAdams, and I liked how she portrayed her character. She was a mean girl, but she had a smile on her face whenever she did it. So I watched all these other things and kind of put some things in and made it creative myself. I just loved playing the mean girl." Ashley actually found that she liked acting like someone totally different than herself. It was a surprise. "I love playing the drama queen," she admitted to the *Asbury Park Press*. "Because that's so not like who I am."

Ashley may not be a drama queen in real life, but with her career taking off into the stratosphere, she was looking more and more like the queen of drama. That's especially true compared to her fellow cast mates, who were all relatively unknown. Ashley quickly emerged as the seasoned veteran on staff, the actress whom the others would look up to the most.

Of all the actors, the one who was probably the greenest was Zac Efron, who landed the part of jock-turned-thespian Troy Bolton. Though Zac played the part of Cameron Bale on the television show *Summerland*, he never considered himself a serious actor. "At this point, when people ask me if I'm an actor, I say I'm a student," Zac told *Teen People*. "Acting has always been a hobby. It's just now that my hobby is taking off. My friends finally get to see what I've been doing all these years." Zac may have been nonchalant about his acting talents, but his looks definitely put him in the star zone. Everyone could see that he is a total hottie!

So if acting was merely a hobby for Zac, dancing was something he'd never even contemplated. "It was tough," he said on *Showbiz Tonight*. "I had no dance experience. I wasn't ready. It was tough, man, it was very tough." And as if *that* wasn't enough, Zac even had to bone up on his basketball skills. "I am *not* a basketball player," he admitted. "I had one real season under my belt, playing with kids who were so much better than me, it was embarrassing. I think I scored two points all season. So it took a lot of practice, to say the least."

The rest of the lead actors were a little better off than Zac. There was Vanessa Anne Hudgens, who played the part of Gabriella. Vanessa was already a member of the Disney family, having acted in the action adventure *Thunderbirds*. For her, starring in *High School Musical* was a dream come true, since it was a chance to dust off her dancing shoes. "I grew up in San Diego, but I'm originally from Oregon," she told *Scholastic News* online. "I'm from a really small town with one stoplight. I used to sing and dance around the house. But there weren't enough people for a dance class. So we moved to California."

Like Ashley, Vanessa has the benefit of positive role models in her mother and father. "My parents have done so much for me," she said. "I started doing singing and dancing in theater and my friend asked me to go on an audition for a commercial, and ever since then I knew I wanted to do this."

Vanessa was actually homeschooled, so unlike her fellow actors, she didn't have real-life experience to draw on with regard to what life in a high school is like. But she adapted well, so much so that her role in *High School Musical* had all the makings of a breakout performance (and, in fact, she appeared in *The Suite Life* alongside Ashley since filming the movie). If Ashley was missing her pal Brenda Song from *The Suite Life*, Vanessa provided a good stand-in. "She is one of my best friends," Ashley told *Tiger Beat* magazine, "which is funny 'cause I'm so mean to her in the movie."

When they weren't filming, Ashley and Vanessa would often squeeze in a few hours of shopping for clothes, having lunch, or hanging out with the other cast members, including Lucas Grabeel, who played Sharpay's brother and coconspirator. Lucas had been working hard in Hollywood since moving there in 2003, after graduating from high school in Springfield, Missouri. He landed the part after impressing producer Bill Borden during the casting call. "He did this little song-and-dance number and had so much personality, I was immediately attracted to him to play this role in our movie," Borden told the *Springfield News-Leader*. At age twenty-one, Lucas was actually the oldest of the movie's main characters, though he had no trouble getting goofy. "I'm committed to getting a laugh," he told the *Atlanta Journal-Constitution*.

The other two actors who rounded out Ashley's posse on set were Monique Coleman, who played math whiz Taylor McKessie, and Corbin Bleu, the Brooklyn, New York—born star of the hit television show *Flight 29 Down* (with the unforgettable head of hair) who handled the part of Chad Danforth, Troy's teammate on the basketball team.

Though the main members of the cast came from different places, they all clicked pretty much immediately. For Ashley, who was used to the strong, family vibe from *The Suite Life*, it was great to work again with such cool people who got along so well. "It was so much fun and it seems like just yesterday that we did it," she told tommy2.net in 2006. "But ya know, it was a blast and we had so much fun during the whole thing. Everybody is, like, ya know, it's like another family besides *Suite Life*. We just kind of bonded and I have all these new friends and we're really excited to see everybody's reaction 'cause for us it's really cool."

Of course, the making of *High School Musical* wasn't just hanging out and having fun. The entire production had to be shot in twenty-five days on a five-million-dollar budget. If that sounds like a lot of money, just think: Some blockbusters can cost around two hundred million dollars and take over a year to make.

Fortunately, the cast had a steady leader in the director, Kenny Ortega. He had worked with even tighter budgets and shooting schedules, so he knew what had to happen to get the movie made. "Our director was amazing to work with," Ashley told KriSeLen.com. "We had a two-week boot camp where we danced from nine in the morning until six o'clock. We also recorded all our music prior to going to Utah, where we shot the movie, and laid down seven tracks in five days, which is amazing because it usually takes more than that."

Some of the actors fared better at boot camp than others. Zac Efron, who's actually had the theme to *Rocky* as his cell phone ring tone, didn't exactly handle it like a champ. "It was Broadway style," he said, describing the regimen to *Scholastic News* online. "We'd wake up at six in the morning and work until six at night. It was a very long day, but by the end, I'd sustained so many injuries and was so sore but so much better than I was before. I learned more in those two weeks than I'd learned in the previous years."

Besides the benefit of learning, Zac also had the comfort of enjoying the company of his cast mates . . . a lot! "That was one of the benefits of being in this movie," he told teenhollywood.com. "Lots of pretty girls." Though there weren't any on-set romances (or so he says!), Zac will admit that "[the cast] immediately became best friends. We got a good group, which is very rare. There wasn't a bad seed among any of the kids."

Once filming began, the cast settled into a regular routine, though Ashley admits that life on a movie set is quite different from what she was used to on *The Suite Life*. "With a sitcom, you have a live audience," she told mediavillage.com. "We go in, we rehearse, we're done by four or done by three, and everything moves quickly. With a movie, they have to get all different shots. You block and then you film it, so it takes a lot of patience. It's a very cool experience."

Despite the endless rehearsals (or maybe because of them!) the set of *High School Musical* had its share of bloopers and practical jokes. "It was like a party every day for us," Ashley told *Tiger Beat* magazine. As for the flubbed lines, everyone seemed to have their own embarrassing story to tell. "I really hope that [they show] the bloopers!" Vanessa Anne Hudgens said to tommy2.net. "'Cause we had some funny bloopers, I must say. Like Zac had one where he was, like, trying to put his shirt on but he couldn't and he took it off and ran back and forth and, like, it was hysterical. So I hope we have bloopers."

But for all the fun and games that they had, the cast members were also working hard, in part because there was a growing sense on set that the movie had something special to it. "There were moments," Monique Coleman, who played Taylor McKessie, told *Showbiz Tonight*. "There were little glimmers shooting a couple of scenes that there's something special going here, specifically the final scene."

Besides the growing optimism that spurred the actors to push themselves harder and harder, filming a movie is just plain difficult. As glamorous as the lifestyle may seem, the days are long and actors are often forced to do difficult things. Ashley, for instance, who loves to walk around in sandals, had trouble adjusting to her character Sharpay's preferred footwear. "I never really liked high heels and I was really scared because she wore high heels all the time," she told teenhollywood.com. That made for some tricky dance numbers, especially "Bop to the Top," which took a full day to get just right (and the song is only a few minutes long!).

Then, of course, there was the scene where Sharpay gets food dumped on her in the cafeteria. Nobody likes that! "It was horrible!" Ashley complained to teenhollywood.com. "It was chili and it smelled so bad. The worst part was that I had to take a shower in the boys' locker room—the *real* boys' locker room." Yuck!

It certainly was an adventurous twenty-five days of filming for the cast and crew of *High School Musical*. But they got the job done and made a few new friends in the process. For Ashley, it was the perfect way to spend her time off between seasons of *The Suite Life*. She probably left Utah for her life back in California thinking that the experience of *High School Musical* was pretty much behind her. Little did she know that the show had only just begun!

Chapter 10

Straight to the Head of the Class

High School Musical had its premiere on January 20, 2006. That was a Friday night, which meant that the movie went up against a lot of other programs targeted at younger audiences. After all, the television executives in charge of scheduling knew that after the long school week, kids love to get together with friends for a few hours of Friday night entertainment. So High School Musical definitely wasn't the only teen-friendly program on the tube that night.

While networks always hope that a new show will attract more viewers than expected, they try to keep their expectations to a minimum. That included the executives at Disney, who went about their weekend like normal, thinking as little about High School Musical as about their own high-school experiences from years ago.

But when they walked into their offices on Monday morning, they were treated to quite a pleasant surprise. Their little movie about life as a teenage thespian had scored huge ratings, attracting over seven million viewers! That was a record for the network and good enough to make *High School Musical* the top-rated, non-sports cable broadcast for the month. It would also go on to earn the highest rating of all movies that ran on cable television in January 2006. You can just imagine the men and women in business suits doing high fives all around as these record-setting numbers rolled in. "We never planned on this," Gary Marsh, president of entertainment for Disney Channel Worldwide, told the *Chicago Sun-Times*. "This movie has taken on a life of its own."

Meanwhile, in schools all across the country, the buzz over *High School Musical* was catching on like wildfire. In the hallways and cafeterias, during homeroom and throughout recess, it was all the kids could talk about. "How cute is Zac?" they gushed, many of them making comparisons to their own high-school hotties. "Sharpay is such a snob! She got what she deserved," others declared, probably drawing worried looks from any It-girl peers within earshot.

The fact that there are so many characters in *High School Musical* that kids can relate to is definitely one reason for the movie's success. "I think these characters are really relatable,"

Ashley told *Showbiz Tonight*. "You've gone to school with our characters. I think they're a little bit exaggerated. But, you know, everyone has a Sharpay and everyone has a brainy girl. It's just actually, like, you relate to it, especially adults do." Chris Byrne, a children's marketing expert, seconded the idea that *High School Musical* is for kids of all ages (and maybe a few adults thrown in). "It's inspirational for younger kids because it's about people they look up to," he told the *Chicago Sun-Times*. "Yet older kids have tuned in because it reflects their social world, touching on what it means to be a stranger."

It's true that beyond the catchy show tunes and scintillating dance scenes, *High School Musical* is very much a story with strong values. The fact that Troy and Gabriella follow their hearts and aren't swayed by peer pressure delivers a really positive message to real kids who might find themselves in similar predicaments. All the actors involved agreed, including Ashley. "The whole movie is about being true to yourself and not being in a clique," she explained to *Scholastic News* online. "You don't have to just be one thing. Kids can get stuck in a clique and can't get out of it. You feel that people won't support you in anything else. I think it's important to find yourself in school and be happy about it. And if people don't support you, they're not your real friends."

Believe it or not, the idea that kids at school can make you feel insecure is something even Ashley has experience with. Even though she would probably be the coolest student at any school, Ashley explained how close to home the movie hit for her. "When I was in school, I kind of went through the same thing," she said on *Good Morning America*. "There's all these cliques and it's really important because everyone can relate, I mean, even older adults can relate because you know these characters so well in our movie. And you know, it's like stepping out of that clique, and feeling like you can say what you are, what else you want to do, and not find yourself after school but [during] school. I think that's really important for kids to learn that. I think it's really amazing. It's a good message."

Zac Efron, who played the part of Troy Bolton in *High School Musical*, views his character's transformation in the movie as ultimately inspirational. "The message from the movie is that you have to be yourself, walk your own path," he told *Scholastic News* online. "Don't listen to all the pressures that come from the outside world. Troy starts out as this hotshot stud, but he's given that name by his peers—it's not really who he is. By the end of the movie, he discovers he can be himself and have just as much fun. He goes through this great transformation. By the end of the movie, he's even cooler." Well said, Zac!

Okay, so everyone thinks the same thing: *High School Musical* has a strong message. Nobody's denying that. But let's face it, there are other reasons the movie developed such a devoted and ever-expanding audience in a relatively short span of time. Consider this: During the six airings between January 20 and February 12, 2006, 26.3 million new viewers tuned in to see this movie! This strategy of repeatedly airing the movie, and gaining a larger audience every time, is new for the entertainment industry. "We live in a culture where it's all about the big opening weekend and nothing else," Chris Byrne said in the *Chicago Sun-Times*. "That isn't what happened here, though. They've allowed it to build slowly by word of mouth, and quite frankly I think it's in a much stronger position as a result." You're not the only one, Chris!

No doubt, *High School Musical* scored big with audiences, but the buzz must have been about more than the movie's positive message and strong core values. So what was it? Well, for one thing, the movie had a terrific sound track. That's something the Disney executives were well aware of even before the movie aired. A few weeks prior to its premiere, they released many of the songs online and offered free downloads of the single, "Breaking Free." Then, just one week ahead of the premiere date, they released the sound track in stores and started showing music videos from the movie on the Disney Channel. That was enough to catch a lot of teenage ears, so the movie had a pretty good-sized fan base to build on even before it hit the small screen.

The early promotions really paid off. In the weeks following the premiere of *High School Musical,* nine songs from the sound track appeared on the Billboard Hot 100 (that's the music industry's weekly list of most-listened-to songs). Just imagine how psyched the cast of *High School Musical* was to see their names next to mega pop stars like Beyoncé, Nelly, and Kelly Clarkson. Or to learn that the band The B5s had done a version of the single "Get'cha Head in the Game," and that the NBA had picked it up as one of its promotional tunes. Slam dunk!

Of all the songs on the sound track, "Breaking Free," the movie's anthem, has probably enjoyed the most success.

In one week it jumped from number 86 to number 4—that's the fastest one-week jump in *Billboard* history! According to Geoff Mayfield, *Billboard* magazine's director of charts and senior analyst, the sound track to *High School Musical* was the surprise hit of 2006. "Album sales have grown every week it's been on the market," he told the *Chicago Sun-Times*. "Even weeks in which it wasn't number one, it still sold more than the prior week. No one saw it coming."

It's not surprising that "Breaking Free" is the most popular song on the sound track, since it really sums up *High School Musical* as a whole. The duet is sung by Zac Efron (Troy) and Vanessa Anne Hudgens (Gabriella), and it's all about how they will achieve their goals if they remain true to their hearts. Another favorite hit is "Stick to the Status Quo," which touches on a similar theme of the perils of peer pressure. Its words are so inspirational that they actually cause one of Troy's sports teammates to admit he loves to bake and aspires only to make the perfect crème brûlée!

Obviously, Disney had met its goal of making a musical that younger audiences would find cool. For Ashley, who was no stranger to stardom after the success of *The Suite Life*, it was an enormous thrill to be a part of such a tremendous cultural event. "The movie's pretty much like *Grease* for our generation," she told *American Cheerleader* magazine. "We sing and dance and break out in song. . . . It's so much fun."

Back in California, Ashley couldn't believe the attention *High School Musical* was receiving—not that she was complaining! "It's crazy. It's, like, it's huge," she told tommy2.net. "I mean, we never expected this much. We knew the movie was gonna be really good 'cause we all can feel that. And we knew it was gonna be fun, and kids would like it. But I think the album coming out of left field and going gold is, like, absolutely nuts. We never imagined that in a million years." Ashley couldn't have been happier. The world realized what she, her costars, and producers knew. She couldn't have summed up the experience any better than when she said, "It's really, really awesome!"

Ashley's other cast mates were just as excited (and surprised) by how well *High School Musical* was doing. "You know it's phenomenal," Vanessa told tommy2.net. "I mean, we knew it was going to be a big thing, but nobody knew it was going to be this big." For the girl from a one-stoplight town in Oregon, the feeling was extraordinary. "Of course I'm just so proud, and it's so great hearing me on the radio. It's phenomenal, really."

Ashley Tisdale

Red-carpet
ready!

Dancing the night away
in *High School Musical*

Ashley
performing
one of her
hit songs
for fans

Ashley and Brenda Song are even better friends than their characters, Maddie and London, on *The Suite Life of Zack & Cody*.

Ashley poses with her sister, Jennifer, and a friend at a Nickelodeon screening.

Ashley looking sweet!

Though Ashley's acting abilities are what landed her the role in *High School Musical*, she's a big part of the success of the sound track. She had already proved her singing chops by performing Broadway musicals for a bunch of years, and now with the sound track, she's thrilled that her talents are reaching a wider audience. It's been quite the breakout moment. In fact, Ashley is one of the only female artists ever to have two songs debut in the same week on the Billboard Hot 100. Needless to say, she's had to pinch herself more than a few times. "I have to say, the weirdest thing was looking at the *Billboard* charts and seeing, like, Beyoncé and Sean Paul and all these people and then seeing Ashley Tisdale. I was, like, *no way!*" she told tommy2.net. "That was just the weirdest thing ever. It was really cool, it was a dream come true because I really wanted to record and do an album one day."

The two songs that launched Ashley to the top of the charts were "What I've Been Looking For" and "Bop to the Top." She performed both tunes with Lucas Grabeel, who played her brother Ryan in the film. Lucas—who moved to Los Angeles from St. Louis, Missouri, in order to make it in show business—was as blown away by his good fortune as everyone else involved in *High School Musical*. He told tommy2.net, "You know the album going gold and all these kids just going crazy and all the iTunes downloads and everything, it's insane."

To get a sense of just how insane it all is, consider this: Even tracks that didn't make it into the movie are turning into hit songs on the radio and online. Case in point: "I Can't Take My Eyes off of You," another one of Ashley's recordings. "It was an additional song written by Matthew Gerrard, who did 'We're All in This Together' [and other songs in the movie]," she explained to mediavillage.com. "He had pitched the song and we knew we weren't going to use it, but we just recorded it, anyway." It's a pretty good sign when even the rejects from a sound track turn into pop favorites, though there's a small part of Ashley that wishes otherwise. "It's kind of weird because it's me and Lucas," she said about doing a strange love-duet with the actor who plays her younger brother, Ryan. "My kid brother is singing it with me and I'm singing 'I can't take my eyes off of you.' But it's a really nice song. It's not really our characters singing."

Though Ashley obviously loves the limelight, her single favorite moment from the filming of *High School Musical* was one she shared with literally hundreds of other performers. "I would have to say [that] the musical number [at the end of the movie] was my favorite because it was so amazing and there were so many people," she said. "There were, like, three hundred extras. It was an amazing feeling. It was the best way to end it and it was like a big party. We were just told to have fun and be happy, and that's just how it turned out."

That sounds like the perfect end to a totally perfect movie experience—lots of people together having fun and being happy. And the number of viewers who are getting in on the good feeling of *High School Musical* continues to get larger every day. The result has been even greater fame and celebrity for Ashley. She gets recognized practically everywhere she goes nowadays. And people constantly approach her for autographs and pictures. "Yeah, they know me as Ashley because [Disney] kind of promotes my name," she told thestarscoop.com. "I just went to a Cheetah Girls concert and I could not believe how many people [were there] . . . I got mobbed. It was unreal. In the amphitheater, they were chanting 'Ashley.' I thought Ashlee Simpson was there, and it was actually me."

Sitting in that stadium with thousands of fans chanting her name, life was pretty sweet for Ashley Tisdale. From that moment in the mall seventeen years ago when she was first discovered through a few star turns on the stage to a leading role on a hit television show and now a starring part in the biggest movie in cable history, her career has only known one direction: up. She may not be quite as big as Ashlee Simpson— not just yet, anyhow. But, everyone knows, it's just a matter of time.

You probably think that with all her newfound fame and celebrity, Ashley has started taking limousines everywhere and eating only at five-star restaurants. But, in fact, she has remained more Maddie than Sharpay. Life may never be "normal" for a mega star, but for Ashley, it's pretty close.

Chapter 11
Keeping It Real

Ashley's just like any regular girl. Yeah, right. Okay, so she's not completely ordinary, but when she wakes up, the first thing she does in the morning is brush her teeth. Well, that's normal, anyway. Seriously, though, now that you have heard all about the fabulous career of Ms. Tisdale the Star, what's it like during a typical day in the life of Ashley?

The first thing to know is that almost immediately after brushing her teeth, she needs a caffeine blast. Ashley's not really awake until she hits her local java outpost of the California coffee chain, Coffee Bean. There, she downs a large vanilla ice blend. It's healthy, though—the tasty concoction is blended with ice and nonfat milk.

Ashley does have to think about fitting into all the latest clothes and looking great on camera (which makes people look a lot bigger than they are), but that doesn't keep her from eating. The Disney star isn't one of those emaciated celebrities who gets filled up by the smell of food. No, Ashley enjoys a good meal. One of her favorite foods is sushi—pretty sophisticated fare. Raw fish isn't everybody's idea of a tasty treat, but in L.A., where Ashley lives, it is as popular as pizza.

Speaking of pizza . . . while Ashley may love fancy food, like sushi, she isn't too good for ordinary junk food, such as gooey, cheesy pizza, which she loves. But out of all the taco shacks, sandwich shops, and other fast-food joints in California, her favorite is the drive-through burger stand In-N-Out Burger. The West Coast chain is not only Ashley's favorite. Loads of other celebrities (and regular people) are crazy for the burgers. There's even a secret In-N-Out menu, for those in the know, including Animal Style (a burger with the works), Protein Style (a burger wrapped in lettuce), or 4X4 (four patties and four slices of cheese stacked between the bun!). Ashley's meal of choice is a hamburger with french fries topped off by a thick chocolate shake.

With all the pressure on young women in Hollywood, Ashley does have to watch her weight. But she has a healthy approach to the whole process. Instead of forsaking food, she eats in moderation and works out to keep her supercute figure. Ashley's routine is to exercise with a professional trainer three times a week. A lot of celebrities use trainers to make the most out of their time at the gym. It's a great way to really make the muscles ripple, if you can afford a trainer's fees.

Ashley doesn't just care for her body. If you are a star, you have to work on just about every aspect of your appearance. But Ashley takes meticulous care of her hair. That's totally understandable—since those long blond tresses are part of her trademark look. But we already know the big secret: Ashley's natural hair is not straight at all. She's got a head full of curls! But she never, ever wears her hair curly, opting instead to straighten it. That can be really hard on the hair's texture. So Ashley has to take extreme measures to make sure she doesn't fry her glossy mane.

"Ashley takes really good care of her hair," her personal and show hairstylist Ozlem Dalgic assured *Sophisticate's Hairstyle* in 2005. "She's really careful about trying to keep her hair in the best condition possible. Using the best products shampoo and conditioner-wise will definitely give you the optimum result when straightening thick, curly hair like that." And that's not all. Ashley keeps a tight lock on split ends. "She gets trims about once every eight to ten weeks and we do deep conditioners at least once a week," Dalgic revealed.

That's a lot of maintenance. Between beauty rituals and learning her lines, how does Ashley find any time to kick back? Recently she moved out of her parents' house in Valencia, California, and into her own condo, which she purchased. That can be a pretty traumatic time for anyone, especially for someone as close to her family as Ashley is. But not only did her best friend and dog move in with her, she didn't move all that far from her family, or from a home-cooked meal. "My parents are just down the block," Ashley told *People* magazine in 2006. "So we'll be eating at their house!"

Still, Ashley is psyched about her new pad. She told the website missoandfriends.com that her house "is the best place to relax." On her days off, Ashley could do anything she wants, but she loves to stay at home and watch movies. Instead of hitting the hottest clubs or restaurants all night, Ashley thinks a great evening is one where she pops in a favorite film and kicks back with a couple of friends. Ashley is nuts for chick flicks, especially ones with marriage themes. Some of her favorites are *Just Married* and *My Best Friend's Wedding*. Hmmm . . . is Ashley dreaming about heading down the aisle? Maybe, but right now she's content to be in the company of her pals, lounging around and watching teen TV on her big screen.

When Ashley isn't checking out her own work on the Disney Channel, she loves to watch MTV, especially *Laguna Beach,* a show that follows the wild lives of eight real teens who live in Orange County, California. "I'm addicted to *Laguna Beach*," she told *American Cheerleader.* "I really love that show."

Don't get the wrong idea. Ashley's not a total TV junkie. Even though she's on it and loves to watch it, she does make time for that good ol' fashioned hobby: reading. Her life is crazy busy, but she curls up with a book whenever she can. "I do like to read. I think it's really important," Ashley told *Scholastic News* online. "It's awesome because it relaxes you. You just put yourself into that book and pretend you're that person in that experience. I read anywhere I can. I love to read in the car. When I'm rehearsing and working, I love to go into my dressing room and read."

Believe it or not, another thing Ashley likes to do during her downtime is something she does for a living. "Singing is something I have always loved to do, so in my downtime I always go back to that," Ashley told the *Miami Herald* in 2005. She also admits to a secret addiction, something you would never expect: knitting! It's much cooler than it seems. Knitting isn't just for grannies anymore. It's become a popular trend among stars such as Julia Roberts and Cameron Diaz. It makes sense that people with lives as insane as celebrities would enjoy a slow activity like knitting. It's also a good way to pass all the downtime on set. Anyway, how cool would it be to get a scarf knit by Ashley?

Ashley has a full life, her own apartment, an amazing job, and great friends. She's pretty much a full-fledged grown-up. But that doesn't mean she can't miss her parents. She does. To make her house seem homier, without her tight-knit clan, she cribs from her mom's recipes. For dinner she told missoandfriends.com, "I try to make my mom's homemade Caesar salad." Hmmm, that doesn't sound too convincing. She also relishes the holidays when they all get together. "I love Christmas, not just because of the presents but because of all the decorations and lights and the warmth of the season," Ashley said on her website, ashleytisdale.com. Her pet dog is never left out of the plans. She is crazy for Blondie, her Maltipoo. "She is sooooo cute!" Ashley squealed to missoandfriends.com.

At heart, Ashley is basically just a big kid. Maybe that's why she conquers her fear of flying by taking either her mother or a stuffed animal (but preferably both) on any plane she boards. Maybe that's also the secret to her success in staying so grounded despite the rush of fame she's experienced. The spring of 2006 brought a flurry of attention. She landed in the pages and on the covers of *Teen* magazine, *People*, *Popstar!*, *Tiger Beat*, and *Bop*. Not to mention all the premieres, parties, and free clothes. "I'm really having the time of my life," Ashley told the *Asbury Park Press*. "Sometimes it's hard to believe it's happening to me." It would be easy for Ashley to forget where she came from and become a major snob. She has people calling out her name wherever she goes. But fame hasn't changed Ashley at all. "It's kind of crazy but I feel no different than I did before I landed my first job," she told teenhollywood.com "I'm still me. I think I'll always be grounded because my parents keep me that way."

One person who isn't ashamed to flaunt Ashley's fame is her grandmother, Marilyn Morris. Ashley and her grandma, who lives in Ocean Township, New Jersey, are really tight. And Marilyn likes to brag about her granddaughter's phenomenal success. She tells all her friends, "I'm Maddie's grandmother." And now, since *High School Musical* has become a hit, she's switched her refrain to "Sharpay's grandmother." The whole thing makes Ashley laugh. "She's been really supportive of everything I've done," Ashley said. "She's really one of my biggest fans."

But don't think her parents, Lisa and Mike, are joining the Ashley cheering squad. Their job is to keep her the sweet daughter they raised. "It's never going to go to my head," Ashley said about her fame to the *Asbury Park Press* in 2006. "My mom would smack me if I ever started acting the diva."

Chapter 12

Future Tense

With such a charmed past and present, it's pretty clear that Ashley has a bright future ahead of her. The success of *High School Musical* is steamrolling ahead. The film pulled in millions of viewers every time it aired on the Disney Channel. With that momentum, the much-anticipated DVD of *High School Musical* arrived in stores May 23, 2006. Who would think that people would want to see Ashley's flick after it repeated on TV about nine times? But they did. Maybe it's because the DVD came in two versions: the original, and a sing-along edition that has lyrics at the bottom of the screen for fans who don't already know every word from watching it a million times. How many karaoke sessions did that spawn?

Vanessa Anne Hudgens loved watching the extra scenes on the DVD, but they did remind her of how much pain those red shoes she wore in the film caused her. "I actually watched the behind-the-scenes version today and I was, like, 'Oh, my God, what was I doing?'" she told teenhollywood.com. "It hurt, but I somehow made it through. I walked in London for miles with these stiletto boots and I survived, so I guess I'm really good with heels."

It's lucky Vanessa has a way with heels because she might just have to put them back on, since a sequel to *High School Musical* is in the works. With the success of the first one, it was inevitable. Producers are smart people who like to make the most out of a good thing. Ashley and Zac couldn't be more excited about the project. They were the first actors to sign on to *High School Musical 2*.

It isn't surprising that Ashley jumped on the opportunity. She's savvy. But when will she find time to fit it all in? Ashley is a hot actress who is totally in demand. She picked up a recurring role in *Kim Possible*, an animated series by—surprise, surprise—Disney about an ordinary high-school student who saves the world after class. And of course there's her role as Maddie in the next season of *The Suite Life,* which starts shooting in the spring.

But Ashley wouldn't let a little thing like scheduling keep her from a part in a big movie. She's got it all planned out. When the second season of *The Suite Life* wraps in October, she has a lot of goals to accomplish—the *High School Musical* sequel, maybe another movie, and what about a concert? Nothing is out of her grasp. Despite all her big dreams, Ashley is still firmly grounded in her Disney sitcom. She wouldn't want anything to get in the way of that right now, or, as she told teenhollywood.com, "I don't want to say good-bye to that yet!"

One thing she would love to do but hasn't yet had a chance to make happen is a project with her sister Jennifer, who is also an actress. "I would love to work with her," she told the *Miami Herald* in 2005. "We did a commercial together, and I would love to maybe have her on the TV show or even do a movie with her. I know it would be fun." Older sis Jennifer is absolutely gorgeous, just like Ashley. Some families have all the luck. While Ashley has a cute, girl-next-door look, Jennifer is the sexy, unapproachable type with very blond hair, very high heels, and very dark eye makeup.

Maybe her vampy look is the reason Jennifer has landed so many parts in seriously scary horror films. She also made a guest appearance on one TV show, *Boston Public*, a Fox drama about the ups and downs of teaching at a high school in Boston. Created by David E. Kelley, the Emmy Award—winning force behind *Ally McBeal* and *The Practice*, *Boston Public* had a long run (for TV, that is), from 2000 to 2004.

Alas, Jennifer only made it on one episode of the drama, but she seems to have more of a knack for the horror genre. In the past four years she's appeared in three gruesome films, starting with *Ted Bundy* in 2002. That was a docudrama— a film that's kind of like a documentary in style and research— based on the real life of Ted Bundy, a notorious serial killer who murdered at least nineteen young women during the 1970s. The film follows Bundy from his college years through mass murder on to his trial. Next up on Jennifer's tour of terror was a part in the 2004 film *The Hillside Strangler*. The title pretty much sums up the entire plot of this slasher film. Just when you thought things couldn't get any darker for fair Jennifer, she landed a part in the 2005 film *Dark Ride,* about a killer who escapes from a mental institution and goes to, where else, a theme park. Sounds like fun. The horror film, which literally had people on the Internet movie sites warning innocent audience members of the freakish violence, also starred Jamie-Lynn DiScala, who became famous playing mob princess Meadow on the HBO gangster hit *The Sopranos*.

Screaming in the woods and running away from

psycho killers—those parts Jennifer played are a far cry from the sweet, wholesome Disney roles Ashley lands. So perhaps before the Tisdale sisters can share a trailer on a TV or movie project, Jennifer may have to lay off the gore.

All this talk about work, work, work. What about extracurricular activities, such as, well, boys? Doesn't a little fun lie in Ashley's future? When it comes to her love life, Ashley keeps her cards really close to her chest. You'll never see paparazzi pictures or read tabloid items about her canoodling with some guy in a club. Everyone wants to see Ashley in love. So much so that the press and various fan sites had her dating her costar, the hunky Zac Efron. Who wouldn't want to date him? Despite the rumor mill and Zac's obvious appeal, the two are not seeing each other. So what is Ashley looking for in a guy? "I look for someone who's really fun to be with. Someone you feel comfortable with and have a good time [with]. Tall, surfer," she joked with teenhollywood.com in 2006. "It's mainly about the personality, though."

Whatever guy she ends up with, Ashley certainly won't rely on him for financial support. This is a girl who loves to work. Luckily she's had tremendous success in the field of her choice. But Ashley says that if she couldn't be in the entertainment industry, she'd be a writer. "I have always wanted to do this my whole life, but I also love to write," she told KriSeLen.com. "I love to write music, scripts, anything! So I probably would be a writer."

Well, Ashley can put the pen and paper away for now. Her acting career is red hot. Ashley's set to take over the entire entertainment industry. She told KriSeLen.com that in five years, she'd like to be "in a TV show still and doing movies, maybe performing in concerts with an album!"

Music has always been a big part of Ashley's life, first through her stint with live theater and then, of course, with her big breakout hit *High School Musical*. Never content to rest on her past achievements, Ashley wants to push the music thing even further by making an album of her very own. Certainly the *High School Musical* CD proved that she has the goods. Ashley has five amazing songs on the *Billboard* charts. "Hopefully it's leading up to recording a CD one day," she told *Scholastic News* online. "I love to write music, and I've been writing a lot of stuff." A lot of stuff is right. Ashley has actually been writing her butt off. That "someday" for the release of her CD might be sooner than you think. "I just wrote twelve songs and am putting together a demo to see who is interested in producing [it for] me," she told the *Miami Herald*. So keep your eyes on those CD racks for an Ashley Tisdale album!

Ashley already has designs on duets with two top singers. "I would love to do a duet with Jessica Simpson. She's a great singer. And Jesse McCartney one day," she told teenpeople.com. Jessica Simpson is actually Ashley's personal role model. Although Ashley is surrounded by famous people almost every day of her life, she is completely starstruck by Jessica. "I think I'd pass out if I met her," Ashley told *People* in 2006. Really, the two girls aren't that far apart. They both are blond. They both can sing, dance, and act. And they both have pet Maltipoos—a breed of dog that's a mix of a Maltese and a poodle—(Jessica's is called Daisy). But while Jessica is on the cover of practically every big gossip magazine almost every week, Ashley is more subdued. "I'm more like the girl next door," she told teenhollywood.com in 2006.

No matter what her other aspirations are, TV remains her first and foremost passion. Being a television star is a dream she's still working on. "*High School Musical* was the first real movie I really did," she told thestarscoop.com. "So I definitely want to do more movies. But I always, always want to have a sitcom. I would love to always have a TV show and then do movies on the side as well. . . . I love TV. My goal is to win an Emmy one day, not an Oscar."

And just as Ashley dreams big for herself, so does she encourage others. Her message has always remained the same. "Don't ever give up," she advised her fans in an interview with the *Miami Herald*. "It is important to pursue your dreams. Don't let anyone, or any rejection, keep you from what you want. Always stick to your goals." Spoken like a true star.

Chapter 13

Ashley's Style File

Now that Ashley has become a superstar, lots of girls her age and younger have had a chance to check out her style. The jury is in: They definitely like what they see. That's because Ashley not only knows how to bend the best of current trends to flatter her own look, she's also a trendsetter herself. With her flowing, fancy tank tops, long hair, chunky jewelry, and cool jeans, she is the epitome of current young fashion. Ashley's hip but not too mature, pairing designer items with everyday mall purchases. *The Suite Life* star takes a nod from one of her personal heroes and style icon Jessica Simpson. "I would take a picture with Jessica Simpson because I love her style!" she told missoandfriends.com. Just like Jessica, Ashley is equally comfortable in a pair of cool sweats and oversized shades, or a girly dress and leather clutch.

Ashley's style is so awesome that it has even influenced the stylists of *The Suite Life* and *High School Musical* when they created her characters' wardrobes. "Maddie is very casual and comfy," Ashley told the *New York Times* in 2006. "Sharpay was way over the top and bedazzled. Her style was based on my Sidekick cell phone, which is pink and sparkly. I'm a mix of both because I love to wear Uggs and leggings and be casual, but I also like dressing up." Well, no wonder the costume designers followed her lead. Now with a few insider tips, you can become a little more like Ashley.

It All Starts with the Outfit

Ashley knows that in order to look good, you have to be the entire package (including a nice person). But like building a house, you must start with a strong foundation. For Ashley, that's the clothes. "I always pick my wardrobe first. Once I have that, I do my hair and then match my makeup," she told *Sophisticate's Hairstyle* in 2005. She doesn't discriminate when it comes to designers, shopping the entire spectrum of cool clothes. Some of her favorite lines include Diesel, BeBe, Urban Outfitters, Betsey Johnson, Abercrombie & Fitch, and Hollister. "My wardrobe stylist on [*The*] *Suite Life* puts all my stuff together from Forever 21," she told teenhollywood.com in

2006. "I love Diesel and I love Urban Outfitters. I just go and look and buy things if I like them."

At this point in her life, Ashley can buy anything that catches her eye because she is a big star with a big bank account. But that wasn't always true, even though she did always love to shop. Ashley never let a lack of funds stand in the way of fashion. She found a way to make money for her shopping habit at a very early age by working in retail while she was growing up. She even worked at the supercute and preppy store Abercrombie & Fitch. "It wasn't fun," Ashley admitted to *People* in 2006. "But I did love getting a discount. Everything I earned went back to whatever store I was working in!"

TiP: A solid wardrobe of high-quality items is the base for any kind of stylish person. No matter how cute your haircut or earrings are, if you pair it with a boring T-shirt and jeans, they will get lost. Shop around for the looks that best suit your body and personality (and, if you're breaking Mom and Dad's bank, use Ashley's example and get a job!).

Don't Be Afraid to Experiment

Ashley is relaxed in everything she does, including her style. "I like to wear sweats and cute T-shirts. Sometimes if I'm going out, I'll wear jeans and a cute top," she told *Sophisticate's Hairstyle*. No ball gown there. In fact, Ashley confided to missoandfriends.com that her coolest article of clothing is "my Juicy Couture sweats that have 'Heiress' written all over them." Juicy Couture is practically required wearing in L.A., where every starlet and starlet-wannabe walks around in the matching tight sweats, clutching a big cup of Starbucks. But recently, Ashley has been taking more risks with her style, having discovered such edgy independent designers as Ed Hardy. And her risks are paying off. "Lately, I've been wearing pinstriped shorts over leggings and I just bought a wide belt that comes up under my chest," Ashley told the *New York Times*. Well, that's one outfit that would certainly get attention.

TIP: Once you've mastered the basics, experiment a little. Having good style isn't just about looking perfect. It's about creating an individual look that gets attention. If something out of the ordinary catches your eye, try it on and take a chance.

A Perfect Head of Hair

Ashley has naturally curly hair but always wears it pin straight. That takes a lot of work. Ashley's personal and professional hairstylist, Ozlem Dalgic, goes through a long process almost every day to create that seemingly natural and effortless look. "We always blow-dry her hair. Then we flat-iron it to give a little bit of extra shine and smoothness," Ozlem told *Sophisticate's Hairstyle*. It's really important to use high-quality brushes, irons, dryers, and products if you are going to put your hair through so many processes. "I do most of the straightening with the bigger round brush. I really do my best to take small sections and get the root of the hair as straight as possible by pulling it with my fingers," Ozlem revealed. "Then I use the straight iron only from the middle of the shaft on down to the ends." Ozlem's last touch is to smooth a little pomade onto Ashley's hair so that no frizzies ever get a chance to pop up. If that sounds like a lot of work, it is. Ozlem gets paid a salary just to tend to Ashley's hair. Nobody, except a star or a zillionaire, can afford that kind of personal attention on their hair. And to do it yourself would take forever. (No matter how much you love style, there are some things more important than spending hours on your hair, like sleeping or eating . . .)

TIP: There are a few shortcuts you can take to get glossy hair à la Ashley. Wash your hair in the evening and use a deep conditioner. Blow-dry it straight and follow up with a pomade or straightening serum. Then sleep on it. Your hair will flatten during the night, mimicking the process of a straightening iron. If you have really curly hair, don't go for the completely straight look. Make braids while the hair is still wet and dry for loose, tousled waves.

Heat's a Killer

Applying high heat on a regular basis can really damage hair. Frequent straightening makes products more important than ever. With Ashley's regimen of intense heat and drying to kill those curls, her products need to hydrate, hydrate, hydrate. "Deep conditioning is essential because I have naturally curly hair and straighten it a lot, so I have to deep condition [it] a lot—otherwise, it's just going to die!" Ashley told *Popstar!* magazine in 2005. To keep Ashley's locks healthy, Ozlem uses PureOlogy Hydrate Shampoo and Hydrate Conditioner. "To protect Ashley's hair and add a lot of shine, I use Schwarzkopf Osis Magic Anti-Frizz Serum," Ozlem added.

TIP: If you can't pronounce *Schwarzkopf*, let alone pay for it, there are less expensive ways to ensure healthy, lustrous hair. During the summer months, when sun and sea can really dry out hair, take a cup of olive oil and in the bathtub pour it through your hair. Leave it on for thirty minutes and then rinse it out (it might take a few times) with shampoo.

Long, Short, Pink, or Blond: Try It All

Everyone knows Ashley as a beautiful blonde on camera. But on her own time, she's a little more adventurous with her hair. She isn't afraid to experiment with different colors just as long as she's ready to be a sweet blonde again when the cameras roll. She's able to do that by using hair extensions—fake hair that is woven into your real hair. The extensions are ideal for actresses because they can come in or out in a jiffy. That's why you see stars with short hair one day and completely long hair the next. Britney Spears is a huge fan of hair extensions. You never know what length her locks will be on any given day.

"Once in a while, depending on what she's wearing and the vibe of it all, Ashley likes to put in different colored extensions," Ozlem told *Sophisticate's Hairstyle*. "We just did a couple of pieces of pink on either side of her hair and it looked fabulous against the blond!"

> **TiP:** It's fun to play around with non-permanent hair dyes to create new and individual looks or to match an incredible outfit. Save up and splurge on hair extensions for a super-special occasion like the prom. Your date will definitely be surprised and psyched when, instead of your usual bob, you have a waist-length mane.

Accessorize, Accessorize, Accessorize

Ashley knows the value of a good accessory. Even her technology is accessorized: In addition to her Motorola Razr cell phone, she carries around a Juicy Couture Sidekick from T-Mobile. That must look hot with her Juicy sweat suit. But Ashley also knows her limits. While her *High School Musical* costar Vanessa Anne Hudgens may be a pro in tall stilettos, Ashley can't stand spiky heels. "I'm horrible in heels," she told *Sophisticate's Hairstyle*. "I have to wear flats. I have the cutest ballerina slippers for dressy events." Whatever it is—jewelry, bags, shoes—Ashley chooses carefully, often splurging on one big-ticket item instead of a lot of lame stuff. She did just that when she bought a Louis Vuitton Globe Shopper Cabas tote (which almost resembles a shopping bag with writing all over it) that she told the *New York Times* was her "first really major handbag purchase." Now that's a huge purchase. But find your own limit.

> **TiP:** Save up for one special item as opposed to spending a little money on lots of little junky items. If it's truly a classy purse or pair of shoes, it will make many different outfits look a whole lot better.

old and New

You can't get much more current than Ashley's style (Juicy Sidekick, hello!). Still, she doesn't discard things that are old. She told missoandfriends.com that her most prized possession is "a charm bracelet from my grandma." Sentimental items are the best, better than the latest hottest trend. Ashley believes that. She wears a Me&Ro leather string bracelet that is a keepsake from *High School Musical*. We already know dreams are important to Ashley, but they even factor into her outfit with a favorite cuff by Dillon Rogers, which reads: "Follow Your Dreams."

TiP: Take a second look at jewelry and other items that come from close friends and family. Although on first inspection they might not seem "stylish," their meaning and the love they come with will transcend any trend.

Chapter 14

Lucky Stars

Ashley Tisdale is certainly poised to give young teen stars like Hilary Duff and Lindsay Lohan a run for their money when it comes to being Hollywood's newest sweetheart, but Ashley is anything but a diva. She could easily be the girl next door or your new best friend, and she has the star sign to prove it! Ashley was born on July 2, which means she's a sweet-natured Cancer. Cancers are known for their patient, gentle personalities and their tenacity and sharpened survival instincts, so it's a safe bet that Ashley will be around for a long time to come.

Cancer is one of the three water signs (along with Scorpio and Pisces) and, like all water signs, Cancers have deeply developed instincts, intuition, and feelings. Cancer's lucky colors, sea green and silver, and precious stone, the pearl, come from the ocean, and, just like the tides, Cancer is ruled by the moon. Water signs know to trust their gut when it comes to making decisions, and they have been known to relax or become stressed based simply on "a feeling" they have about a situation or event. Ashley knows to rely on her superstrong intuition, and it hasn't failed her yet. Basing her career moves on her instincts about certain parts have led her to portray characters suitable for her age and personality instead of rushing into racier and edgier roles like some of the other Hollywood starlets her age. Ashley has been more comfortable establishing herself as a talented, wholesome young actress and easing into more mature roles—and so far, it's working. After all, whether she's playing a lovable sweetheart or the girl you love to hate, Ashley is irresistible!

Cancers have a bad reputation for being crabby and moody, thanks to the ocean dweller that symbolizes this sign: the crab. Ashley is as far from crabby as you can get, but she does share some of the crab's more lovable qualities. Crabs have hard shells that protect them from predators, and Ashley has developed a thick skin of her own in the years she's been working in showbiz. Auditioning for part after part means a lot of rejection, but Ashley has a hard shell of dreams and a firm belief in herself to get her through all the "nos." Like most Cancers, Ashley is very driven and always has her mind on the future and what she wants to accomplish. Being super-dedicated to her goals and dreams means that Ashley always has something to strive for and look forward to, giving her the discipline to keep working hard even when it isn't easy. The crab's hard shell is part of the reason that crabs have been around for over five hundred million years, and tenacity like Ashley's means she'll probably outlast a lot of other stars her age. She's a survivor, and that's just fine with us—we can't wait to see her in future roles!

Underneath that hard shell, Cancers are very sensitive and loving. They are family oriented and treat their friends like an extension of their family. Ashley is certainly close to hers—she moved out to be on her own, but only a few blocks away! And that's far enough for her for now. Cancers like the feeling of being safe and protected with the people they love. They also tend to prefer to stay home and relax instead of going out partying all night. Ashley's favorite way to unwind with her friends is to kick back at home with a movie and yummy snacks, in true Cancer fashion. Ashley and her sister are the best of friends, and she'll never pass up one of their mom's home-cooked meals. But Ashley has created family for herself outside of the family she was born into. Working on *The Suite*

Life of Zack & Cody has given Ashley a new sister in Brenda Song and little brothers in Dylan and Cole Sprouse. Ashley loves taking care of her friends and costars and, like all Cancers, she is very nurturing. She's the first to offer a hug when someone is having a bad day or make someone who's sad smile with her goofy antics. And, of course, Ashley uses her Cancer intuition to give great advice to her friends and family, just like other famous Crabs—"Dear Abby" and the Dalai Lama!

Cancers tend to be shy and sensitive, and Ashley wasn't always the outgoing sparkler we know and love today. She credits cheerleading with helping her get over her shy nature—but we think she was just born a star! Because Cancers can be sensitive and get their feelings hurt easily, they are always careful to be mindful of others' feelings and like to make sure that everyone is happy and having fun. Cancers often get a bad rap for having mood swings, but smart Cancers like Ashley know that this can work to their advantage. They feel things deeply and know their emotions in and out. Ashley is able to channel this into her acting. She can portray emotions realistically because she feels everything so deeply.

Cancers are also known for being great comedians and performers once they come out of their shells—which explains why Ashley has such a gift for comedy. Ashley even uses her childhood clumsiness to help her fall naturally when performing physical comedy. Cancers have sharp minds and great memories, and Ashley is no exception. Her fantastic memory helps her memorize lines and dance numbers quickly. She can even play a song on the piano after hearing it only once—talk about talent! Ashley is also extremely smart and hard-working, pushing herself relentlessly to achieve her dreams. That's one powerful combination: talent and drive—no wonder she's such a success!

When it comes to love, Cancers are very picky. They prefer a mate to be one of the other water signs, like a fellow Cancer or a Scorpio or a Pisces. Cancers need someone sensitive and stable who will make an effort to get under their shell and truly understand them. Aries can be too harsh for Cancers, and Aquarius is too wishy-washy, making either a bad match. Cancers like Ashley tend to take their time finding the right person, but when they do, it's often an intense and long-lasting bond.

Ashley hasn't been linked romantically with any Hollywood hotties yet, but when she finds the right guy, we'll know because she won't be able to keep her happiness from showing. Cancers long for true love and never give up hope of finding their soul mates, even if they don't talk about it openly. Once in love, Cancers are fiercely loyal and protective, providing their mate with security and comfort. Cancers are often private about their deepest desires and most personal feelings, choosing to protect and nourish them until the perfect moment. This tendency means that people are often surprised by Cancer's accomplishments because they don't see them coming until the last minute.

Ashley, like the crab symbol of her star sign, is one tenacious chick. She's smart and intuitive and never gives up on the things she truly wants and works for. She plays up her strengths and has learned how to turn her weaknesses into helpful qualities—channeling her sensitive emotions into her acting abilities and her stubbornness into an unstoppable work ethic. Ashley would clearly go far no matter which sign she was born under, but her Cancer instincts and drive to survive certainly help. It's her Cancer sweetness, loyalty, and kindness that have made her into the Hollywood sweetheart we just can't stop watching!

Chapter 15

By the Numbers

1	2	3	4	5	6	7	8	9
A	B	C	D	E	F	G	H	I
J	K	L	M	N	O	P	Q	R
S	T	U	V	W	X	Y	Z	

Ever wonder what gives a celebrity that elusive star quality? The answer could be in his or her name—and it can be found using numerology. Numerology has been practiced by mathematicians since Galileo's time and it's still used today by celebrities and nonstars alike, to determine how their name can affect who they are.

Numerology uses the relationship between the letters in a person's name to determine specific characteristics of that person's personality. Each letter in the name is matched up with a particular number from a numerology chart. The numbers are then added up to reveal that person's master number. For example, Ashley's full name is Ashley Michelle Tisdale. By matching the numbers from the numerology chart to the letters in her name, "Ashley" is 25 or can be read as 7 (25 is broken down to 2 plus 5). "Michelle" is 40 or 4, and "Tisdale" is 25 or 7. The numbers are then added and the total is 18, which can then be broken down to the single digit of 9. This 9 reveals the truth behind Ashley's beautiful name. As a 9, Ashley is intuitive, creative, a born businesswoman, and a dreamer—with an amazing ability to see the big picture and to become a leader in her community.

It's easy to see why Ashley is a 9! Her career as an actress has been fueled by her creativity and intuition for choosing just the right roles. As a 9, she knows to trust her instincts, and it's clear she does. Sure of how she'd like her career to progress, Ashley accepts only roles that she feels will propel her in that direction. She's held on to her good-girl image by choosing roles—such as Maddie on *The Suite Life of Zack & Cody*—that are close to her own personality. But now that Ashley has established herself, she's beginning to branch out into more demanding roles. In *High School Musical*, she played Sharpay, the popular and mean drama queen—quite a stretch for sweet Ashley! She embraced this role because it was different from anything she had done before. She was ready for the challenge.

Ashley is a born businesswoman, but her "business" is her acting career, which she handles like a pro. Ashley has resisted the temptation to give in to the Hollywood pressure that says she must look like every other waif actress onscreen. She hasn't embraced a racier, more sexual image because that isn't who she is or wants to be. Ashley knows that trends come and go, so she strives to be a classic performer—one who can handle any part and isn't stereotyped into one specific type of role. Ashley is an exception in young Hollywood, taking only roles that she thinks will give her career staying power and momentum. As a 9, Ashley is always looking at the bigger picture. She avoids shock-value parts and chooses roles with substance instead. She doesn't want just her fifteen minutes of fame . . . she's planning on fifteen years of fame—or longer!

As a 9, Ashley seeks to improve the world around her. One of the reasons she's been eager to portray "good-girl" characters is to be a positive role model for her fans. Ashley attended regular school growing up, missing only a few days at a time to film commercials, so she knows what it's like to deal with peer pressure, growing pains, and finding your own identity. Ashley loves playing Maddie on *The Suite Life* because Maddie is a lot like her—an average girl who is a good friend, a hard worker, and who always tries to do the right thing in every situation. Maddie also attempts to teach London, the snobby heiress character on the show, how to become a better friend and a less selfish person. Fans of the show have an excellent role model in Maddie, and in Ashley. Ashley goes out of her way to attend many Disney events so she can interact with her fans and encourage them in person. And she chooses to dress stylishly in an age-appropriate way, even when she isn't on TV or making an official appearance—to help young girls realize that you don't have to wear too-tight clothes or show skin to be pretty. In a pop-culture-saturated world that encourages girls to grow up too fast, girl-next-door Ashley is a breath of fresh air for her fans.

Sometimes, 9's can be accused of not paying enough attention to details, but, while Ashley has a tendency to focus more on the bigger picture, life's little details don't escape her! Ashley handles finances with finesse, making smart purchases such as a condo and a car, instead of blowing all of her money on lavish parties or a closet full of designer duds. Ashley is always stylin', of course, but she does it on a budget—picking up her clothes at less expensive stores like BeBe and Abercrombie & Fitch, instead of high-end designer shops.

When it comes to style, Ashley is all about the details. You'll never catch her out and about without serious accessories. She loves to complete her look with the perfect bag or pair of shoes. She doesn't go overboard with baubles, but what she does choose makes a statement. How else could she appear on so many Best-Dressed lists? And you have to be patient and pay close attention to details with a beauty regimen like Ashley's. Ashley's naturally dark, coarse, curly hair has to be deep-conditioned, straightened, highlighted, and infused with lots of beauty products to keep it looking so luscious. Ashley has perfected her overall look by planning down to the tiniest details, which is pretty sweet!

Ashley is definitely a 9 when it comes to being a dreamer. She knew what she wanted from an early age and never gave up on her dream of becoming a star. She's worked tirelessly on multiple commercials, television appearances, and guest roles to get where she is today—and she couldn't have done any of that if she didn't have a clear vision of her dream to keep her motivated. Ashley believed in her dream so much that she bargained with her parents to give her a year to pursue acting full-time. If she didn't make it, she said, she'd then go to college and choose another career. Ashley knew that she had what it takes to succeed. She wasn't going to let anyone—even her parents—keep her from going for it. Now that she's finally a small-screen star, her dreams can only get bigger and better, which means we can expect plenty more from Ashley in the future.

Numerology isn't an exact science, but it can often provide valuable clues about people's strengths, weaknesses, and overall personalities. In Ashley's case—with her creativity, intuitive nature, and business smarts—numerology shows that she was born to be a star. But it was Ashley herself who made her dreams come true. Numerology just gives us a better picture of the girl behind all the glamour.

Chapter 16

Are You an Ashley Expert?

How well do you know Ashley Tisdale? Take this quiz to find out!

1. Where was Ashley discovered?

2. When is Ashley's birthday?

3. Where was Ashley born?

4. What was Ashley's first acting gig?

5. What is the name of Ashley's character on *The Suite Life of Zack & Cody*?

6. What is the name of Ashley's dog?

7. What is Ashley's zodiac sign?

8. What was Ashley's character's name in *High School Musical*?

9. In what show did Ashley make her Broadway debut?

10. What was Ashley's favorite class in school?

11. What is Ashley's favorite color?

12. What is the food Ashley can't live without?

13. Who is Ashley's favorite actress?

14. On *The Suite Life of Zack & Cody,* Ashley plays a candy-counter clerk, but what was Ashley's real life high-school job?

15. What is Ashley's favorite TV show?

16. What top actress did Ashley work with in a T-Mobile commercial?

17. Who is Ashley's favorite solo artist?

18. What was Ashley's least favorite thing about filming *High School Musical*?

19. What was Ashley's first big purchase after landing her gig on *The Suite Life of Zack & Cody*?

20. What was Ashley's favorite activity when she was growing up?

Answers:

1. Her local mall; 2. July 2, 1985; 3. New Jersey; 4. A commercial for JCPenney; 5. Maddie Fitzpatrick; 6. Blondie; 7. Cancer; 8. Sharpay; 9. *Les Misérables*; 10. Creative writing; 11. Pink; 12. Sushi; 13. Jessica Simpson; 14. A Wet Seal salesgirl; 15. *Laguna Beach*; 16. Catherine Zeta-Jones; 17. Billy Joel; 18. Wearing high heels all the time!; 19. A condo; 20. Cheerleading

Chapter 17

Internet Resources

Ashley is a star who continues to shoot higher and higher. We know this girl isn't going to spend all her days lounging by the pool or shopping, no matter how much she adores those activities. We're talking about the actress who films movies in between TV shows! Her career is on the go, and she's loving every minute of it. By reading about how much happened to her in 2005 and 2006, you can see how quickly her world is changing. So if you want to stay on top of Ashley's latest news, head online and check out the following websites. They will definitely keep you current on everything happening in Ashley's life. You should always get a parent's permission before signing online, and keep in mind that websites are always coming and going!

Ashley's official Website

www.ashleytisdale.com

Ashley Tisdale Fan Sites

www.ashley-tisdale.com

www.ashley-tisdale.org

www.ashley-tisdale.us

www.ashleytisdaleconnection.com

Internet Movie Database

www.imdb.com/name/nm0864308/

TV.com

www.tv.com/ashley-tisdale/person/12106/summary.html

Chapter 18

The End of the Beginning

Ashley has only just begun a career that is sure to be long and successful. How could it not be, with Ashley's talent and determination? Luckily for her fans, Ashley isn't in any hurry to go anywhere. She's taking it one day at a time and pursuing more of the fun projects America has grown to love her in. As she progresses and evolves as an actress, there will most certainly be edgier projects and more demanding roles, but we'll always love Ashley most as the good-natured sweetheart she is underneath all the makeup, hairspray, and Hollywood glitz—and we know you will, too!

PRICE STERN SLOAN
Published by the Penguin Group
Penguin Group (USA) Inc., 375 Hudson Street,
New York, New York 10014, U.S.A.
Penguin Group (Canada), 90 Eglinton Avenue East, Suite 700,
Toronto, Ontario, Canada M4P 2Y3
(a division of Pearson Penguin Canada Inc.)
Penguin Books Ltd, 80 Strand, London WC2R 0RL, England
Penguin Ireland, 25 St Stephens Green, Dublin 2, Ireland
(a division of Penguin Books Ltd)
Penguin Group (Australia), 250 Camberwell Road,
Camberwell, Victoria 3124, Australia
(a division of Pearson Australia Group Pty Ltd)
Penguin Books India Pvt Ltd, 11 Community Centre,
Panchsheel Park, New Delhi - 110 017, India
Penguin Group (NZ), Cnr Airborne and Rosedale Roads,
Albany, Auckland 1310, New Zealand
(a division of Pearson New Zealand Ltd)
Penguin Books (South Africa) (Pty) Ltd, 24 Sturdee Avenue,
Rosebank, Johannesburg 2196, South Africa

Penguin Books Ltd, Registered Offices:
80 Strand, London WC2R 0RL, England

Photo credits: Cover: courtesy of Eddie Malluk/WireImage.com. Insert photos: first
page courtesy of Jeffery Mayer/Star File; second page courtesy of Jenny Maki/
Shooting Star and Stephen DeFalco/Shooting Star; third page courtesy of Glen
Harris/Photorazzi and Jemal Countess/WireImage.com; fourth page courtesy of
Eddie Malluk/WireImage.com

Library of Congress Control Number: 2006028055

Special Markets ISBN-13 978-0-8431-2667-9; ISBN-10 0-8431-2667-1
Not for resale

zac attack

An Unauthorized Biography

by Grace Norwich

zac attack

An Unauthorized Biography

by Grace Norwich

PSS!
PRICE STERN SLOAN

contents

introduction

Up for the Challenge

To be a teenage superstar in today's world, where hit shows like *American Idol* and *The O.C.* mean that just about everyone is vying for a piece of the action, you need a few things going for you. Being adorable definitely helps. Having an awesome body doesn't hurt, either. But let's face it: There are almost three hundred million people in this celebrity-conscious nation of ours (never mind Canada and other countries, where a lot of stars are born). That means a ton of pretty faces and hot bods. Most schools—heck, most *grades*—have three or four prizewinning specimens.

Put Zac Efron in any high school in the world, and he would definitely be a candidate for the best-looking award. That mop of brown hair, with the sweeping bangs and sideburns that curl down cutely past the ears, might remind you of a young Ashton Kutcher. Zac's deep blue

eyes, meanwhile, are somewhere between Brad Pitt's and the late, great James Dean's. As for Zac's body, he's nothing short of the full package—abs, bis, tris, you name it.

Still, there's more to Zac than good looks and a firm physique—all five foot, ten and a half inches of it. The French have an expression, "*je ne sais quoi*," which basically means "something you can't quite put your finger on." In English we have another term: star quality. Whichever language you prefer, Zac's definitely got it going on. The guy practically oozes attitude.

But attitude, as you frequently see in Hollywood, can take a turn for the worse. How often do you hear about stars losing their cool, punching out some paparazzi, or partying a little too hard? Zac's attitude, on the other hand, is always positive. For one thing, he's probably the healthiest heartthrob on the planet. He starts out every day with a long, hard jog, and, as much as he likes the ladies, he's said he wouldn't even consider going on a date with one who doesn't treat her body like a temple, the way he does. As proof, Zac told *People* magazine in June

2006 that "smoking would be the thing that would make an impossible match for me."

To go along with his focus on fitness, Zac also keeps a totally healthy perspective on life. His parents had a lot to do with this, constantly encouraging Zac to take on new challenges, from singing to dancing to horseback riding to skydiving (which he hasn't tried yet, but really wants to!). The lesson Zac learned was that if you're afraid of failure, you'll never get anywhere in this world. "It's important to make sure you go out and try new things as often as you can," Zac explained to the *Plain Dealer* in 2006. "You've got to do what feels right for yourself, and don't let your friends decide for you. You have to realize your real friends will stick by you whatever decisions you make."

More than his leading actor looks, it's this "try anything" approach to life that explains Zac's success. While you may look at him now and think he's a born performer, Zac actually had to work really hard to get past his natural shyness. The story of his break into acting says it all. "I was actually forced by my dad into my first musical,"

he told *PBS Kids*. "My dad convinced me to go out and audition. I said yes, thinking it was a few months away and I'd somehow talk myself out of it by then. Little did I know it was the next day!" Can't you just imagine the look of terror on eleven-year-old Zac's face when his dad broke the bad news? Zac continues: "So I went into this audition kicking and screaming, and little did I know my dad had just showed me the coolest thing on earth. He opened so many doors for me."

Once those doors were opened, there was little stopping Zac. From bit parts in musicals to a recurring role in a hit television show to the lead role in the biggest movie in the history of the Disney Channel, Zac's star has enjoyed a steady and at times exhilarating ascent.

Through it all, the blue-eyed cutie has remained remarkably unfazed. It's often said of the best performers—whether actors, athletes, musicians, or politicians—that they make the job look easy. That's the case with Zac. When you watched *High School Musical* for the first time, did you ever think that Zac was once lousy at dancing and

even basketball? Well, he was! During the height of the *HSM* hysteria, Zac appeared with his castmates on *Good Morning America*. The reporter asked about Zac's abilities on the basketball court. "Oh, my [skills] are nothing like they are in the movie," he confessed. "I'm not that great at all. I had one year of Little League basketball and I did so bad. I think I scored two points all season."

Pretty hard to believe, isn't it? Yet somehow, Zac makes audiences believe. It's the fact that Zac is true to himself and up for any challenge that gives him the power to play other people so convincingly. More than his terrific smile and fantastic hair, these are the gifts that make Zac Efron a superstar.

This willingness to take chances is the one thing Zac wants to pass on to the millions of fans who have come to love and adore him. As he told *TeenTelevision*: "My advice to teens is to try and do something that scares you every day because it's the only way you can test how far you can really go; whether it's going out and auditioning for the play or trying out for the basketball team, you have to

explore your boundaries and see where you really want to go, and the only way you can do that is to break out of your shell." So *breaking free* isn't just the name of the hit song that helped make Zac famous. It's also a way of life!

chapter 1
The Early Years

Zachary David Alexander Efron was born on October 18, 1987, in San Luis Obispo, California. It should come as no surprise to hear that Zac was a pretty cute infant. "He was a beautiful 'Gerber' baby," Zac's dad, David Efron, told *J-14* magazine. "He cried if you left him alone, and he loved to be held."

The house Zac grew up in is actually in Arroyo Grande, a quiet, sun-soaked village on the Pacific coast about halfway between Los Angeles and San Francisco. It's a small, tight-knit community, with about seventeen thousand residents spread out over five-and-a-half square miles. The streets are pretty and lined with trees, while the houses are modest and well-maintained.

There's definitely an all-American vibe to Zac's hometown. Ambling through Arroyo Grande's historic

downtown district, with its charming array of antique shops, family style restaurants, and mom-and-pop businesses, you practically feel like you're on the set of a Hollywood movie from the 1950s. It almost looks *too* perfect. Not that anyone complains! Even people who don't live in Arroyo Grande tend to love it, especially during the springtime, when the town hosts its annual Strawberry Festival. This fun-filled event draws thousands of visitors from all over the region for a few days of games, crafts, and of course the endless sampling of strawberry treats.

Arroyo Grande also has an excellent school system. In fact, Arroyo Grande High School really isn't that different from the one featured in *High School Musical*, the movie that made Zac a household name. It has about twenty-six hundred students. In addition to studying hard (the majority go on to college), a lot of the kids play for one of the school's many sports teams, which include baseball, soccer, swimming, and basketball. The school mascot is the eagle, and the sports uniforms are blue and gold. All in all, Arroyo Grande High has a lot of strong school spirit.

It's no wonder that Zac's parents decided to raise Zac and his younger brother, Dylan, in this idyllic, kid-friendly California community. "It's nice and warm, the perfect town for me to grow up in," Zac told *Tiger Beat* in 2006. Close your eyes and you can picture Zac, along with a pack of pals from the neighborhood, riding their skateboards or dirt bikes through Arroyo Grande's quiet streets, maybe stopping off for milk shakes at the ice cream parlor (though if Zac was as big a health nut then as he is now, he might have insisted on a snack from the local farmer's market!).

Growing up in such a carefree community definitely had a positive impact on Zac. He was about the most easygoing, well-adjusted kid you could ever hope to meet. "Outgoing, gregarious, fun, and very comfortable around adults" is how Zac's dad described him in the *J-14* magazine interview. Zac was also able to play the part of the fool every now and then. "He was in his fifth-grade class working with scissors and he accidentally cut off one of his eyebrows," his dad told *J-14* magazine. "He decided

to make the other match. He really got teased about that by his classmates."

In addition to growing up in a great town, Zac had the benefit of a happy home life, and for that he has his parents to thank. It's sad to say, but there are a lot of stories in the tabloids and glossy magazines about parents of hot young celebrities behaving badly or treating their children more like employees than their own flesh and blood. Fortunately for Zac, his mom and dad have always been the loving, nurturing types. That goes for Zac as well as his kid brother, Dylan, who is four years younger—though you wouldn't always know it from the way they interact! "I treat [Dylan] like he's my age," Zac explained in *Popstar!* magazine. "As my dad says, I love to stoop to his level."

Despite the age gap, Dylan, who is the athlete of the family, has clearly been a strong influence on his actor brother. If nothing else, he's a constant sparring partner, always keeping Zac on his toes. Here's how Zac described a typical afternoon at home in *Popstar!* magazine: "[Dylan] will just come over and tap me and I'll sort of push him

back and he'll shove me back and then I'll knock him back and then he'll push me until I fall over and then I'll get up and wrestle him to the ground—we're just brothers. We goof off and inevitably we fight! We have to fight, it's just in our blood, and I think we have the most fun when we're fighting." Boys will be boys!

Zac and Dylan also like to engage in the occasional practical joke, often at each other's expense. "[The other day] Dylan made me reach into a dark, scary hole to look for a golf ball he accidentally threw in," Zac told *Teen* magazine. "When I put my hand down there, he screamed, 'SNAAAAAKE,' at the top of his lungs. I almost passed out. He laughed." So much for the baby of the family being afraid of his older brother!

Even if the Efron household got a little wild at times, Zac's parents definitely knew the meaning of the word *discipline*. David Efron is an electrical engineer (he actually met Zac's mom at the power plant where they were both working at the time), so it's safe to assume that things like education and hard work are a big part of the

Efron family values. "I was always sort of a bookworm," Zac confided to *Twist* in a July 2006 interview. "I always tried to get the best grades, and I'm proud of that. In my family, if you got a B on your report card, it was, 'Shame on you.' It was a blessing, because that attitude stuck with me through high school." At one point, Zac actually boasted a 4.3 grade point average, even with all the advanced-placement courses his folks encouraged him to take!

Despite the challenges of being a showbiz student, Zac has had as much success in school as he's had onstage and in front of the camera. His dad, for one, isn't surprised. "When Zac really wants something, he can be ruthless in his pursuit," he told *J-14* magazine.

Zac has obviously had a lot of very positive influences in his life. There's one final factor that helped shape Zac as a person: his star sign. Zac's October 18 birthday makes him a Libra. Now, you may not be one for astrology, but a lot of the traditional traits that describe Libras sound like they were written specifically with Zac in mind. For one thing, Libras are often very good-looking people. Does

that sound like someone familiar? Second, in addition to being beautiful themselves, Libras also appreciate beauty in others, which means they tend to be on the romantic side. It's no secret how fond Zac is of the opposite sex! Third, Libras are very social beings, and they tend to get along well with all sorts of people, not just the ones they have things in common with. That pretty much describes Zac in a nutshell. "In high school I really didn't have a clique," he told *Life Story* magazine. "I was more of a floater. I tried to hang out with everyone. I had friends in all the groups."

Clearly, the stars were aligned when Zac entered into this world. Throw in the great hometown that he was lucky enough to grow up in and the parents who raised him so well, and it's no wonder he's had such a charmed life. Still, nothing in life is just handed to you. It would still take that courageous first step into the spotlight before Zac could begin to realize his true superstar destiny.

chapter 2
Taking the Plunge

Different kids reveal their talents in different ways. A future star athlete might show early signs of balance and coordination while someone destined to become a famous clothing designer will likely develop an early fashion sense. We already know that Zac Efron was a very outgoing child. But it was the way he always seemed to be humming a tune that made his folks think they might have a natural-born performer on their hands.

As Zac explained to The WB.com, "When I was younger, my dad noticed that whatever song came on the radio, I would sing along with it, and that I could carry a tune, which was really different than anyone in our family, because no one in our family had ever sung before."

In fact, although both of Zac's parents enjoy listening to music, no one in his family had been much of

a performer. At one point, Zac thought his grandmother had been in the circus, but that turned out to be an exaggeration. "I actually found out that was sort of a fib on my part, because she wasn't in the circus," Zac said in *Life Story* magazine. "She was in some kind of traveling group, but not the circus. The picture I found was just of her on Halloween!" Oops! Sorry, Grandma!

Still, even if Zac's parents weren't trained entertainers, they knew enough to keep a close eye on their firstborn's talents, which were developing fast. "I used to sing the Tin Man song from *The Wizard of Oz* at, like, three," Zac said on *CompuServe TV*. "As I got older, I sang my favorite songs from the radio. My parents heard I had a good voice and they encouraged me. They both love music."

But as much as Zac enjoyed singing along to his favorite musicals, he wasn't exactly begging to get up in front of a live audience of strangers. Mom and Dad were persistent, however, realizing better than Zac did that what he really wanted was to perform. When the local

theater group announced it would be staging a production of *Gypsy*, the hit 1950s musical by famed lyricist Stephen Sondheim, they strongly encouraged Zac to give it a shot.

"My parents thought that I should go in and try it," Zac explained to *CompuServe TV*. Zac, who was only eleven years old at the time, thought otherwise. "I had a horrid time," he said. "I was not excited about auditioning for it." But much to his surprise (and horror!), he landed the part of the newsboy. Though it was a small role, once Zac got a taste of the spotlight, you couldn't have dragged him away from it. "From day one, I got addicted to being onstage and getting the applause and laughter," Zac admitted to the *San Luis Obispo Tribune* in 2006.

Gypsy ran for ninety performances, each one more exhilarating than the last for Zac. From there, he went on to appear in probably forty or fifty musicals, including *Peter Pan*, *Auntie Mame*, *Little Shop of Horrors*, and *The Music Man*. Good times were had by Zac on all the productions, but *Peter Pan* was probably the most fun. "I loved playing John in *Peter Pan*," Zac told *Newsday* in July 2006. "That

was a really fun part because I got to fly around on a 'fly' wire. I was hovering over people in the audience. I actually knocked off a guy's toupee once."

Looking back, you can see that it makes perfect sense Zac would get his start in showbiz through musicals, since they're what he grew up watching as a kid. When asked by *TeenTelevision* in 2006 what his single most favorite movie musical was, Zac replied, "Definitely *Grease*. I also love that show *Singing in the Rain*. It's so great, the energy and the dancing." Zac was especially moved by Donald O'Connor, who played the comical role of Cosmos Brown, best friend to Gene Kelly's lead character, Don Lockwood. "Brilliant," Zac said. "Everyone has to go watch that movie. It's so magic." Zac was so into that musical, he admitted to *PBS Kids* that he's watched the same scene from *Singing in the Rain* "probably fifty times in one night, laughing harder every time." Obviously, Zac's appreciation for musicals runs deep!

Even now, when aspiring actors ask Zac what they can do to break into show business, he always points them

in the direction of the stage. "I would definitely say do theater," he told *Teen Dream*. "The way you catch the bug and fall in love with this business is to do theater. It's so nice to be in front of an audience and feel their energy. It really sparks your passion. There is no better way to learn skills—go out and try theater. Local theater is everywhere." (If you want to take Zac up on his advice, check out the Internet for community theaters in your area.)

As much as Zac credits theater with jump-starting his career, he always sensed that there was a bigger world beyond the local stage. From the age of eleven on, he started taking more intensive singing and dancing lessons. Once he reached middle school, he also started taking drama classes at school. That decision would prove to be the most fateful, since it was his eighth-grade drama teacher who persuaded Zac to pay a visit to Hollywood. "The teacher had an agent in Los Angeles and she recommended me to go down and meet them," Zac explained to *Teen Dream*.

So Zac made the three-hour drive to Los Angeles

to meet with a few big-time Hollywood agents. There's no telling how nervous he was that day, but he obviously played it cool since the meetings led to his first professional television part!

Things were really starting to happen for Zac, but the success wasn't going to his head, in part because his parents remained so involved in his life. Zac's mom, for instance, assumed the role of personal chauffeur. "Three times a week she drives me back and forth from San Luis Obispo to Los Angeles," Zac explained to *Popstar!* in 2006. His dad and brother, Dylan, meanwhile, were always waiting for him at home (though after a long day of auditions, there must have been times when Zac wished his prank-playing kid brother would get lost!).

More than ever, Zac would need the parental guidance and stable home life. That's because in the coming months, life was only going to get crazier.

chapter 3
On the Rise

Despite his obvious gorgeous good looks (a must in Hollywood) and his hardworking nature, it wasn't easy for Zac to break into show business in the beginning. All that driving back and forth from home to LA without any success took a toll on Zac's positive attitude. He remembers the feeling of his first audition—and his first rejection—for the 2003 film version of *Peter Pan*, directed by P. J. Hogan and starring Jeremy Sumpter as Peter Pan. "I'd never done a movie audition before, so I didn't come prepared at all," he told *Tiger Beat* in 2006. "I didn't get the part, but it was a reality check." What kind of reality check, though? Zac could have easily thrown in the towel and told himself he just wasn't good enough. But luckily, that wasn't his conclusion. "You have to do your best every time. But after each audition, you have to forget about it,"

he explained to *Tiger Beat*. "You always have to be looking forward and not looking back."

And that's exactly what Zac did: He kept on trying. It paid off. In 2002, Zac landed his first guest appearance on a TV show. He got a role on an episode of *Firefly*, a futuristic show about humanity after it abandons Earth, that ran for a season on Fox. Zac played Young Simon in the episode called "Safe," which aired on November 8.

That was just the beginning of a stream of roles on TV shows. In 2003, Zac landed a plum part in a comedy pilot, *The Big Wide World of Carl Laemke*. All the major television networks order pilots, or test episodes of a new show, to see if they like how an idea pitched in a boardroom actually looks on the small screen. Every year, the big studios and networks order way more pilots than will ever actually get on air. Unfortunately, that's what happened to this pilot, where Zac was set to play the title character's son, Pete Laemke. It never came close to making it on TV.

Despite that minor setback, the guest appearances kept on coming. The same year as his failed pilot, Zac was

on the award-winning hospital series *ER*. The following year, he was on one episode of a CBS show, *The Guardian*, about a hotshot lawyer who ends up becoming an advocate for underprivileged children.

Zac kept trying like crazy to get a meaty part. In 2004, he went out for an audition for a part that could really test his acting abilities. Zac was actually one of the last actors to try out for *Miracle Run*, a Lifetime TV movie based on a true story of twin brothers with autism. He read for the part of one brother, Steven Morgan. He came prepared and nailed it. "I was so happy to get the role," he told *Life Story*. "I got the call and they asked me to do the movie. Within the next day or two, I flew out and began shooting in Louisiana and it was amazing."

Amazing is right. In the TV movie, which filmed in LA, New Orleans, and Atlanta, Zac acted opposite Emmy award–winning actress Mary-Louise Parker, who played Corrine Morgan, the mother of the autistic brothers. Autism is a developmental disability that affects normal brain function and presents itself in the areas of

communication and sociability. In Corrine's case, one of her sons can't talk, while the other can only copy other people's conversations. After Corrine's boyfriend kicks her family out of the house, the boys are almost institutionalized. But the family sticks together. With encouragement from their mom to do "normal" things like play sports and do chores (and a lot of sacrifice on her part), the brothers eventually become students in a regular high school—an astonishing achievement that made for an uplifting story.

Zac—whose onscreen twin, Phillip, was played by actor Thomas "Bubba" Lewis—took inspiration for his role from a kid he knew growing up. "I actually pretty much had the character when I went into the audition," Zac told *Young Star News* in 2005. That's because Zac decided to mimic someone he had known over the years who wasn't autistic but had strange and different mannerisms. "I was always sort of imitating him in my mind. Basically I did an impression of him."

Like the conscientious student he is, Zac also read up on autism to prepare for this challenging role. He dove into

Thinking in Pictures: My Life with Autism by noted autistic author and speaker Temple Grandin. He didn't have much time to research since filming began quickly after he landed the part, but Zac told *Life Story*, "After a few chapters, I was more educated than the average person by far on autism." Knowledge is one thing, but acting rests a lot on emotion. Zac had that down as well. "I tried to just think about how each scene would go through their eyes. That's something every actor does. It's what you've got to do. How would the situation look from their perspective and their shoes?"

Miracle Run premiered August 9, 2004, and instantly received critical acclaim. Zac was nominated for a Young Artist Award for Best Performance from a Supporting Young Actor in a TV Movie. "Efron and Lewis are commendable in their performances for not resorting to stereotypes of the developmentally disabled," Ann Donahue wrote in *Variety* in 2004. "Each gets his moment to shine with a savant talent, giving the story the foundation it needs to wrap up with an optimistic finish." That's pretty high praise for a bunch of newbies!

The kudos didn't come just from the critics. Famed actor Aidan Quinn—who played *Miracle Run*'s Doug Thomas, Corrine's eventual love interest and a father figure to the twins—praised Zac's fantastic performance. Quinn was especially interested in *Miracle Run* and had a lot of sensitivity to the issues at hand because he has an autistic daughter. "I was kind of amazed at the job they did," Aidan Quinn said of Bubba and Zac in the *San Bernardino County Sun* in 2004. "In a short period of time, they learned certain looks, ways of walking and holding their hands—things that are particular to autistic kids that, when you're the parent of an autistic child, you know inside out."

Miracle dealt with heavy topics, but of course it had its lighter side. "I wouldn't confine it to the autism aspect," Aidan told the *U-SGV Tribune*. "It's also a whimsical, funny film. We had a gas making it."

Zac had a blast as well, and he made a pal for life. "Bubba Lewis is a good friend of mine to this day," he told *Life Story*.

His career was definitely on a roll. But with all this

work, Zac's schoolwork became an issue. Although he's always been a great student (remember, he kept up a 4.3 grade-point average!), running to LA all the time to shoot his TV shows made it hard to keep up with public high school in San Luis Obispo. "It's difficult trying to go back and forth between work and school," he told *CompuServe TV*. "If I go down to LA to work, I miss a whole day of school. Then you're mailing all your schoolwork back and forth to your teachers, and it gets complicated." Zac would have to figure it out—since the parts didn't stop. By 2005, Zac had three years of professional acting under his belt. During this time in his career, he was still getting mostly guest roles like one on *CSI: Miami* for the episode titled "Sex and Taxes" (can you picture sweet, innocent Zac in a show with such a racy title?). But as it turns out, one of these guest appearances would turn out to be Zac's big breakout role.

chapter 4
Ups and Downs

The entertainment industry is notoriously fickle. One season a show is the hottest thing on television, the next it's unexpectedly yanked off the air. Actors, too, have to suffer through these highs and lows, landing dream parts one day, only to be told a week later that their character's suddenly been "eliminated." For Zac Efron, *Summerland* was the show that would teach him this valuable lesson once and for all.

Summerland was the brainchild of Lori Loughlin, who some fans will remember from her role on *Full House*, the popular 1990s sitcom that made world-famous celebrities out of Mary-Kate and Ashley Olsen. Loughlin had created an honest, true-to-life drama set in a hip California beach community. She would play the part of Ava, a successful fashion designer in her thirties whose main

focus is her career. That is, until her sister and brother-in-law are killed in a sudden car crash and she's left to raise their three young children.

Enter a trio of rising young stars. The biggest and brightest was Jesse McCartney, who played the part of sixteen-year-old Bradin Westerly on the show. McCartney's heartthrob status was already in place thanks to the years he'd spent singing in the boy band Dream Street and later as a solo musician. Next came Kay Panabaker, the beautiful, whip-smart actress who was chosen to fill the role of twelve-year-old Nikki Westerly. Talent obviously runs in Kay's family: Her sister is Danielle Panabaker, who's been in a bunch of television programs, including *The Bernie Mac Show*, and even appeared opposite Paul Newman and Ed Harris in the movie *Empire Falls*. Rounding out the *Summerland* cast was Nick Benson, who was awarded the part of eight-year-old Derrick Westerly. Nick appeared in the feature film *National Treasure*.

Summerland first aired in the summer of 2004 on the now-defunct WB channel (you see, even entire

networks can get killed at any moment!). From its opening episode, the show established a kind of cult following. It may not have been on in every living room in America (in fact, far from it), but those viewers who did tune in were instantly hooked—no doubt instant-messaging their friends about this and that scene even before the episode ended.

The story of the three young Westerly kids uprooted from their quiet country home in Kansas and sent to live with their wacky aunt on the West Coast made for compelling television. "One of the things that made our show what it was is that we portrayed real," executive producer Remi Aubuchon told *Life Story* magazine. "The audience felt that we weren't trying to give them a lecture and we weren't trying to make everything cool." He and the other producers wanted to make sure the characters were living through typical things that happen to real people. "Then see how they solve their issues," Aubuchon said. "In a sort of unique, fun, 'lots of beach' way."

Summerland definitely confronted its share of issues, whether it was Bradin's adolescent angst or Nikki's

conflicted feelings toward her aunt-turned-mother-figure, Ava. But the core characters could only carry the drama so far. Eventually, the show's writers had to introduce some supporting roles to keep up the momentum. Sitting around the writers' table one day early in the first season, one writer came up with the idea for another teenage character named Cameron Bale. They would make him fourteen years old so that he could fit right in the middle of Bradin and Nikki—able to interact with both characters. He'd be this sweet kid from the neighborhood but with depth, not to mention his own share of darkness. Oh, and just for fun, he would be really, really cute. The other writers loved the idea, and Cameron was written into the next episode.

But what actor would they get to play the part? He couldn't be a huge star, yet he had to have star potential. He had to have boyish good looks but also a soulful side. Sound like someone familiar? Zac definitely thought so. From the moment he heard about the part of Cameron Bale, he knew he had to have it. Remember what Zac's dad said about him being so ruthless when he really wants

something? Well, you can just imagine how passionately Zac lobbied for an audition with the *Summerland* casting agents. Eventually, they granted him a tryout. Zac nailed it in every way.

"I went into the audition," he told *Life Story*. "Two weeks later they gave me a role, and this was after only one audition." Just like that, Zac was set to appear on one of the hottest shows of the summer. At first, his character was slated for only one or two episodes. But Zac was so good in the part of Cameron Bale and got along so well with his castmates that the writers decided to reconsider. Zac explained, "Before *Summerland*, everything I had done was just a guest-starring role and you don't really get to know the cast when you're there for just a day or two. Then when *Summerland* came along, I was just a guest star at the time, but slowly I became part of the cast."

After years of endless auditioning and countless near misses, Zac had finally gotten his first big break. In no time, he was elevated to a regular character on *Summerland*. Sparks began to fly almost immediately as Zac's character

and Kay Panabaker's character discovered they might have more than just neighborly love. "The first scene I ever did on the show was a make-out scene with Kay," Zac told The WB.com. "Those are really tough, but everyone made me feel right at home. It was a blast because we got it out of the way. It made me feel like a part of the cast."

Once he was fully accepted on the show, Zac really started to understand how comfortable working as an actor can be. "Everything is completely different when you're around people like that," he said about the *Summerland* gang to *Life Story*. "They're like your family. And when you get to know everybody, it's more like hanging around with a bunch of friends. It's much more relaxed."

Though Zac got along famously with everyone in the cast, he was probably closest to Jesse McCartney. That's despite the fact that their characters were often at each other's throats! The two could often be found playing pool together or just hanging out. They no doubt talked a lot about Jesse's career as a singer, which Zac found really inspiring, though he admits he was also a little awed by

the more established boy-bander. "I'm actually pleasantly surprised that no one's been holding me up to Jesse's standards, because there's no way I can fill those shoes," he told *Popstar!* magazine in 2006. "He's incredible. He's the boy right now. He's replacing boy bands by himself. I don't think I can be near his caliber anytime soon. I'm working at it, but Jesse's a step above everyone right now."

In addition to learning about the life of a singer from Jesse, Zac was always getting tremendous insight into his chosen profession. "I really got to see what acting is like," he reflected in *Life Story*. "It was a great break into the business. . . . I got to build a family with the people at *Summerland*. I would see them three days a week easily, and there's a strange feeling that comes with being on a TV show, and I got to feel what it was like and feel it out and test the waters."

Season one of *Summerland* ended on a high note for the entire cast, especially Zac. His character, Cameron, had been firmly elevated to "regular" status, and the writers were looking forward to developing it even more seriously.

Zac was wildly upbeat during the break from filming. He admitted to The WB.com that during that time, he was "all about the drama. This season, we find out that [my character] has some really deep and heavy issues. His father is an alcoholic and he's been abused. My plan is to run with that and bring in some drama, the kind that *Summerland* has seen before." Zac knew it would be pretty difficult to play such a tortured soul, considering his easygoing past and loving family. But he was up for the challenge. "Luckily, I've never had to deal with the kind of intense pain he's had to deal with," he told The WB.com. "That makes it exciting for me. I really get into trying to imagine what it's like to be in someone else's shoes."

Unfortunately, even as Zac was preparing for his expanded role, the network executives were setting into motion the show's cancellation. It was another case of "hot one season, gone the next." There are lots of theories about why *Summerland* didn't go far. But probably the most valid is that by opening the second season in the dead of winter (January 2005), it gave fans a major case

of the chills. After all, it's a little hard to relate to a show about a bunch of people frolicking on the beach in swim trunks and bikinis when there's a blizzard blowing outside your window!

Whatever the reason, *Summerland* was officially yanked from the lineup in April 2005. Zac remembered the moment he got the bad news. "I got a call from a good friend, who is Lori Loughlin's publicist," he told *Popstar!* magazine. "Lori was on the line, too, and they said, 'Zac, are you sitting down?' and I said no, even though I was! I was actually playing video games. There was a big, awkward silence and then they said, '*Summerland* is canceled.' I had a feeling, but part of me didn't think it was gonna happen because Jesse McCartney's the coolest thing since sliced bread. So I had high hopes." But alas, the execs in charge felt differently.

Summerland had given Zac his single biggest showbiz experience to date. But in the course of a phone call, that was all ancient history. Not even a star as big as Jesse McCartney could keep the show from succumbing

to the fickle forces of the entertainment industry. But as disappointed as Zac was, he had learned a very valuable lesson: When you fall off the horse in Hollywood, the only thing you can do is get right back on. Considering the storyline of Zac's next project, that lesson sure was an appropriate one.

chapter 5
Riding onto the Big Screen

E ven if it doesn't win him an Oscar, an actor's first feature film is always a formative experience. For one thing, making movies is a really different process than performing onstage or doing television. Think about it. While plays and TV programs can go on for years and years, a movie is usually shot in a few short months. That makes for a much more intense experience.

That intensity is multiplied many times when one of your costars weighs over a thousand pounds and runs almost forty miles an hour! That was the case for Zac Efron when he landed a starring role in the film *The Derby Stallion*.

The story centers around Zac's character, a fifteen-year-old kid named Patrick McCardle, who's from a small country town and has trouble fitting in with the rest of the world. His dad is a former pro athlete, but Patrick

isn't good at sports, so there's plenty of tension there. And Patrick isn't very good at making friends with other kids in town. In fact, his only pal is a gentle old man with a lot of bad habits—drinking and gambling, mainly—named Mr. Jones.

One day Jones introduces Patrick to an injured racehorse he owns. Shortly after, Patrick befriends a couple of newcomers to town, a brother and sister named Jill and Chuck from the nearby city. Together, the unlikely foursome bands together to try to win the coveted State Cup Steeplechase. The movie has all the ingredients of a good story, including a couple of bad apples named Ronald and Donald who are intent on making life miserable for Patrick and his newfound friends.

Of course, Zac was thrilled to be tapped for the part. But looking back, he realized he didn't really know what he was getting into. "I've never done any horseback riding," he told *Life Story* magazine. "I assumed when I signed on for this movie that it was all going to be done by stuntmen. Then the first day when I came on set and

talked to one of the producers, he said, 'Yes, you have three lessons and you're going to be jumpin'!' I guess that really turned on my adrenaline."

As we've already seen, Zac's entire life until then had been about taking on new challenges. So he had no trouble getting up on that horse. "I started focusing 24/7 on horseback riding," he told *Life Story*. "They had one of the greatest teachers come in and help me. Previously, horses were never something I thought I'd be interested in. The first time I got on the horse, I realized I was completely wrong. It's a different experience, and at the same time, it's fun! It's so thrilling and amazing to be on top of a horse."

After just a few lessons, Zac looked like he'd been riding horses his entire life—even though it came with a lot of bumps and bruises. "Oh, man, it was some of the worst pains I ever had in my entire life," Zac admitted to *Young Star News* in 2005. Still, some of Zac's costars had it even worse. Mike Nardelli, who played the part of a spoiled rich kid, said in the same article, "I've fallen off the horse twice, while Zac has not fallen off—yet."

Besides learning how to ride a horse, Zac and his castmates, many of whom also hailed from California, got to experience what life is like in rural Georgia. Much of the film was shot on location in and around Barnsley Gardens Resort, which is about an hour north of Atlanta. It's beautiful countryside, with lots of rolling hills and wooded areas.

The cast seemed to really enjoy the setting. "It's a nice change of pace from LA, with all its traffic and smog and all the people and everything," Mike Nardelli said in *Young Star News*. There were, however, the occasional moments of country-style excitement. As Colton James, who played another of the town's ne'er-do-wells, explains, "One time we actually had to do another take because there was a shotgun shooting in the background!"

Even with the occasional gunshot, the filming of *The Derby Stallion* was pretty calm. Zac was extremely grateful for the chance to learn what goes into the making of a movie. He also got to play a character with a bit of depth and darkness, which is great because he was denied

the opportunity to do this on *Summerland.*

For the most part, though, the few months spent in Georgia represented a pretty quiet period in Zac's life. But knowing what was about to happen next, a little rest and relaxation in the country was exactly what he needed!

chapter 6
Disney Makes a Musical

When veteran producer Bill Borden came up with the idea to make a *West Side Story* kind of musical for today's teens—one that would appeal to both boys and girls—he had no clue he'd have a hit on his hands. "I wanted to make a film that didn't speak down to anyone," Borden told *Newsday* in 2006. The idea was nothing less than brilliant.

Still, nobody wanted it. He had shopped the old-fashioned musical idea around for a year without any luck. "I couldn't get anywhere," he told the *Los Angeles Times*. That was until he went to Disney, where they went crazy for the concept. They set him loose to make his movie.

To write a story that would captivate today's discerning youth, who are more used to Green Day than *Singing in the Rain*, Borden enlisted Peter Barsocchini, a

former music-journalist-turned-screenwriter. Barsocchini's knowledge of music as well as his professional writing abilities were the perfect mix for the task at hand. It didn't hurt that the writer also had a twelve-year-old daughter, so he had a really good idea of what kids want from their entertainment. For his part, Barsocchini wanted to create a musical that would address peer pressure and how to resist it. "High school is such a polarized time," Barsocchini told the *Courier Mail* in 2006. "You've got the jocks and the brainiacs, the goths, the drama geeks; everyone has preconceptions about each other." He wanted to break down those labels through his story and the music.

The story that would become *High School Musical* definitely takes a nod from Shakespeare's famous play *Romeo and Juliet*, the seminal drama about young people in love despite huge odds stacked against them. Add to that a touch of *Grease*, John Travolta and Olivia Newton-John's seventies classic movie that brought together two high-school students from very different worlds, all to a rockin' sound track. Mix the two together and voilà, you've got a pretty cool movie.

In *High School Musical,* a cute, athletic guy named Troy Bolton meets and falls for a brainy (but of course adorable) girl, Gabriella Montez, while both are on vacation. During a New Year's Eve party, the duo find themselves center stage singing karaoke, much to their chagrin. Later in the story, Gabriella transfers to Troy's school, East High School, where she discovers he's a total jock—the captain of the basketball team, even! Gabriella is more the nerdy type (yeah, right), competing in scholastic decathlons. They connect again and get it into their heads to try out for the leads in the school musical. But everyone disapproves—Troy's teammates, Gabriella's bookish gang, and last but not least the performing siblings Sharpay and Ryan, who are used to snagging all the best parts for themselves. Talk about obstacles! Romeo and Juliet had it easy in comparison!

"The result in the story is that when the star of the basketball team admits he wants to sing onstage, it turns the school upside down," Barsocchini told the *Courier Mail.* "Don't judge a book by its cover. Don't typecast people."

Seriously, if that's not a super-positive message, what is?

Once the storyline was down, famed choreographer and director Kenny Ortega jumped on the *HSM* bandwagon. Ortega was the perfect choice to bring this project to life. He had choreographed the cult films *Dirty Dancing* and *Ferris Bueller's Day Off*. Ortega had also directed some episodes of *The Gilmore Girls*, which is a huge hit with teens. His pop culture credentials were definitely up to snuff, but Ortega, who was mentored by the late screen idol Gene Kelly, also had a classy background.

Ortega was really inspired by the message behind *HSM*. "I like the idea of young people coming to know their own voice, regardless of pressure from peers, teachers, parents, and society," he told the *Courier Mail*. "Too much bullying goes on and as a result kids back off from new ideas they have about themselves." He was also happy to introduce a new, younger generation to musicals. It hasn't exactly been a hot genre. "Young people don't get too many musicals," Ortega told *Newsday* in 2006. "That's what I thought was really fun about this, that we could go back

and borrow from the classics, not reinventing the wheel, but do something for young people today."

HSM felt like a mission to all these guys—it was not just another movie. "I wanted to do something important," Ortega told *Life Story*. "I didn't want to do just another Disney Channel film."

Zac, who had grown up doing musical theater, was totally psyched when he heard about *HSM*. And he could completely relate to the character of Troy, a cool guy who follows his own heart. In fact, it was all the performing, singing, and dancing Zac did as extracurricular school activities that gave him that Troy-like perspective. "I was sort of in the same boat as Troy when I was hanging out at school," he told *TeenTelevision*. "Everyone thought it was so cool to be part of the basketball team, but to go out and be in plays at the local theater houses wasn't that cool, I guess. But it would be really fun to have your friends come and watch the shows because then they could see what the heck you're doing all this time when you're missing school and aren't able to hang out." A lot of times Zac had

to stand up for himself and his interest in theater, despite what all the other kids were saying about it. He knew he had to follow his true passions and not the crowd.

But that's basically where the comparison between him and Troy ended. The rest was acting. "We're as similar as we are different," Zac told *Media Village*. "Troy is like the star at his high school. He's a basketball stud and hotshot. I was not like that when I was in school. But the way he is around people is like me." Zac claims that he was a nerd in high school, although that is so hard to believe. It's more likely that he's just being shy and self-deprecating. But the young actor insisted that compared to Troy, he was a loser. "He gets all the cool girls. He's like the dream character to play," Zac told *PBS Kids*. "Every guy would like being more like Troy when they were in high school. I wish I was more like him."

A lot of other young actors got wind of *HSM* and turned up for the auditions, which were especially grueling. The producers and director decided they wanted to cast a bunch of relatively unknown teens, not big-name stars.

"We're not famous kids," Efron said, describing the crowd to the *Chicago Sun-Times* in 2006. "This was just a bunch of newcomers who were trying something."

Zac's musical theater background gave him a leg up when it came to the audition. He was used to the sweat it takes to make something look right on the stage. "I had it easier than some guys at the *HSM* audition—some of them were passing out!" he told *Scholastic News*. "It was Broadway-style, seven-and-a-half hours of dancing, singing, and acting. And then we had to play basketball. I was probably weakest at that."

Zac, who chose "Let Me Love You," by Mario, as his audition song, was quickly paired up with actress Vanessa Anne Hudgens, who was trying out for the part of Gabriella. Vanessa had some Disney experience under her belt, having starred in the movie *Thunderbirds*. But this audition had some added anxiety for her. Poor Vanessa. In going for Gabriella, she was up against a lot of her friends who wanted the same part. The pressure was on, and there was basically no time to practice! "There were hundreds of

us auditioning," Vanessa told the *Edmonton Sun*. "It was nerve-racking."

It didn't help that Vanessa didn't prepare any music to sing for the audition. "I spaced out and forgot I was trying out for a musical," Vanessa told *Entertainment Weekly* in 2006. Whoops. Well, she came out of it like a pro and ended up performing an a cappella version of Kelly Clarkson's "Low."

Zac was glad he was paired with Vanessa because they made a connection immediately while auditioning. "We were put together from the beginning," he told *TeenTelevision*. "To some degree, I think that helped us out because we really got to know each other."

Their chemistry mimicked the relationship between their characters, Troy and Gabriella. "There's people that you just click with right when you first meet them," Vanessa told *Popstar!* in 2006. "Gabriella and Troy just look into each other's eyes and feel comfortable. It's just like sweet puppy love!" What about between the real-life actors? More dish on that later.

He had the background, the smokin' body, and the great auditioning partner, but Zac still had no idea if he would get the part or not. The jitters clouded any perspective he might have had. "We were just nervous," Zac admitted to *TeenTelevision*. "I don't think any of us knew. The people that did know or did think they were great were the ones that immediately got let go because they were so overconfident. It was the nerves that actually saved you."

After a long and nail-biting process, the list of thousands of candidates was finally whittled down to just fifteen different actors auditioning for each role. The tension shot through the roof. They had to dance, sing, and act their hearts out for the Disney executives and movie director. "As they watched, they would tap people on the shoulder and send them home, saying they were no longer needed," Zac told the *San Luis Obispo Tribune*.

Zac never got that tap on the shoulder (neither did Vanessa, who beat out *American Idol's* Diana DeGarmo to score the part of Gabriella), but he went home without

knowing who did get the part. The producers couldn't decide between Zac and one other boy. It was the longest week and a half before he got the call that would change his life forever. Zac landed the part of Troy.

Now it was time to meet the rest of the cast.

chapter 7
The Friendly Set

After the crazy trial Zac went through to get the part of Troy in *High School Musical*, he knew Vanessa Anne Hudgens, his auditioning partner, pretty well. But what about the rest of the *HSM* folks? Zac would have to wait until Utah, where the movie was shot, to meet the other actors.

Well, almost. Believe it or not, Zac already had a friend on the cast. Ashley Tisdale—the perky blond star of Disney's sitcom *The Suite Life of Zack & Cody*—and Zac were pals way before either of them found out they made it on *HSM*. In the musical, Ashley got the part of Sharpay Evans, the high-school drama queen who hogs all the parts for herself and her brother. Sharpay couldn't be further from super-sweet Maddie, the character Ashley plays on *The Suite Life*. As soon as Ashley discovered she was set to

play Sharpay, one of the first things she did was dial up Zac. Ashley was so excited, she screamed into the phone, "I booked it! We're going to Utah!" The two flew on the same plane, sitting next to each other in first class like bona fide celebrities (no champagne, of course).

In real life, Ashley's definitely not a bully. But she didn't mind acting like one. "It's cool to play a character that isn't like me at all," she told *Teen People*. In order to tap into the maximum meanness she needed to play Sharpay, she watched the ultimate movie for just that purpose. "I watched Rachel McAdams in *Mean Girls* for inspiration," she told *Teen People*. "She does mean things but always has a smile on her face."

Lucas Grabeel, a native of Springfield, Missouri, was tapped to play Sharpay's equally mean brother, Ryan. At first, Lucas wasn't that keen on *HSM*. "I thought the script was kind of generic," Lucas told *Entertainment Weekly* in 2006. "Once I met Kenny Ortega, I was like, 'This may actually be something cool!' " Good thing he didn't blow that chance. Lucas found some commonalities between

him and Ryan. "I'm like Ryan because I have a strong background in theater and I did a lot of performing while growing up," he told *Newsday*.

The *HSM* producers made sure they'd filled their hottie quota when they enlisted Corbin Bleu to play Chad Danforth, Troy's best friend and fellow jock. Born in Brooklyn, New York, Corbin was totally psyched to play Chad, since he normally got cast as a nerd (certainly not because of his looks). The cutie who started out as a child model compared himself to his character. "Chad is a very passionate person about everything he does, which is something we have in common," he told *Newsday*. "Where we are not alike is that Chad is not open to new things. I love change."

That's good—since Corbin's life, and the lives of all the actors, was about to change a lot, especially the day in the summer of 2005 when they began the process of making *HSM*. Disney had given the producers a modest budget of five million dollars (that's a lot of money to most, but not in Hollywood terms). Although the story is

set in Albuquerque, *HSM* was actually shot over twenty-three days in Salt Lake City, Utah. Director Kenny Ortega chose Salt Lake City because it was familiar territory. He had done the choreography for the opening and closing ceremonies of the Winter Olympics held there in 2002 (for which, by the way, he won an Emmy).

On the first sweltering day, the cast and crew gathered to embark on the most intense training of their lives. In two short weeks, they would all have to get up to snuff in singing, dancing, and acting (oh, and for some, sports as well). They had a top-notch team in place to guide them, but there wasn't a lot of time. "We didn't know what we were doing," Zac remembered thinking that first day (according to *Popstar!* in 2006). "We were thrown into a dance room and there were mirrors everywhere! We didn't know anything about each other and had to learn these dances."

The schedule was super-intense. For those two weeks, Zac and the rest of the cast would start practicing around 9 A.M. and spend the entire day doing exercises for

singing and dancing. "It was really tough because I'm not a dancer," he told *Media Village*. Luckily for Zac and the rest of the gang, Disney hired dance star Charles "Chucky" Klapow to help with the choreography. By the time he was ten, Chucky (also the grandnephew of a Rockettes' choreographer) had mastered tap. He quickly added jazz and hip-hop to his repertoire. By age twelve, he was so good that Patti LaBelle, Celine Dion, and Salt-N-Pepa had hired him as a backup dancer. "He's awesome," Kenny Ortega said of Chucky to the *Daily News of Los Angeles*. "He is a master in the making. His creative instincts, coupled with his technical know-how, love for the work, and winning personality make him, in my opinion, the new choreographer to watch." Good thing, since Chucky had to direct the one hundred and thirty dancers in the finale.

The pressure on Zac to dance for a Disney film was made even greater when Kenny and Chucky enlisted the finest dancers in all of Utah to perform with him. They learned the routines at the same time. Needless to say, it took Zac a little bit longer than these trained

professionals. More bluntly put, he told *Popstar!* in 2006, "It was pathetic."

As if dancing wasn't hard enough, as soon as he got done with that, it was straight to the basketball court. No loafing around or grabbing candy from the craft service table. Zac had to tackle yet another area—playing hoops—that he didn't exactly shine in (remember how he scored only two points during an entire season of basketball?).

The producer hired a professional basketball coach to put the boys through their paces. "We'd run basketball practice as any basketball team would," Zac told *TeenTelevision*. "We had to run suicides and all get in the layup lines and we'd run several drills."

Corbin has been dancing since he could walk, and he loved combining that with acting. But playing basketball? That was a different story. "Dribbling through the legs while dancing was so hard!" he told *Popstar!* magazine. "There were so many times when I would just start losing the ball." No kidding. While they were filming "Get'cha Head in the Game," everyone kept on getting hit with basketballs by mistake!

Zac didn't get done with all his rehearsing until 5 P.M. at the earliest. By then, he was dog-tired. "At the end of the day, I just remember being so beat and beyond tired," he told *TeenTelevision*. "I reached a new level of sleep every night. It was crazy." All that work really took a toll on the young actors' bodies. Vanessa's feet killed her because she had to do a lot of her dance scenes in really tall heels. Zac—who we know wasn't the greatest dancer when he started out—twisted his ankles, pulled muscles, and got shin splints. He had to chug Gatorade and pop a lot of aspirin to make it through the rehearsing. "I got all beaten up," he told the *Dallas Morning News* in 2006. "But it was all for a good cause."

Zac's costars ribbed him about his two left feet and lame hoops skills. Ashley said Zac did have the hardest time learning the dance routines, but she gave him props for sticking it out. "Zac wasn't the best dancer in the world or the best basketball player," she told *Newsday* in 2006. "Seeing him onscreen, he looks like the best basketball player and the best dancer." He did look *great* onscreen,

but sometimes it took him a bunch of times to get it right. In one scene where Zac had to run into the gym and put his shirt on like he was just getting dressed, it took him three times to do it the way he was supposed to! You might wonder why, since this wasn't nearly as hard as a big dance scene. "My mike kept falling out of my shirt," he said with a laugh (according to the *Plain Dealer* in 2006).

For Zac, the best part of doing *HSM* was definitely the great friends he made along the way. With such a big cast and crew, there was always a lot of boisterous fun to be had. Who wouldn't have fun if you get to dance while working? The *HSM* shoot was basically like summer camp. That included a lot of practical jokes. "All of us did our share of pranks," Zac told *Tiger Beat* in 2006. Zac played one on his pal Corbin when he decorated his dressing room with a lot of caution tape. When Corbin walked in to change, he saw the place covered in CAUTION! He knew the culprit right away and started chasing Zac around the set.

The pranks, the hard work, and all the hanging out created a major bond among the *HSM* actors. "We were

very close," Zac told *TeenTelevision*. "We're all very tight still to this day." To cool off during the long, hot days making a movie, they swam at the Grand America Hotel's pool. On their days off, they went sledding down the Alpine Slide in Park City or visited the planetarium. "We sat by the pool and we ate at every restaurant within five miles," Zac told *News for Kids*. They never left anybody out of the plan, so when they'd hit the local restaurants, there would always be sixteen people. And they all wanted to sit at the same table! "People would think we were absolutely crazy," Zac told *Popstar!* in 2006. The producers definitely facilitated the fun by hosting club nights where Zac, Ashley, Corbin, and the rest of the cast could get down.

Everyone involved in *HSM* knew they had something special on their hands. People had such a good time making the film, they figured some of the joy would have to come out on the screen. But of course they didn't *really* know how it would all turn out. Zac told *Life Story*, "The cast and crew were very excited the whole time we were making it, and that came through on camera."

Saying good-bye to all the excitement wasn't easy for anyone. When it was time to go home, everyone was super-sad, kind of like the last day of camp. "It was so hard not to be able to go to the hotel room next door and knock," Zac told his website zefron.com. "If I could go back and do it again, I'd do it in a heartbeat."

chapter 8
An Unparalleled Success

When *High School Musical* premiered on January 20, 2006, nobody anticipated what was about to happen. Zac and his crew blew everyone and everything out of the water. The *HSM* premiere on the Disney Channel, with 7.7 million viewers, broke a network record. But that was only the beginning of the stratospheric ride. Eventually, a whopping thirty-six million viewers saw the gang sing and dance their hearts out over twelve broadcastings (and out of those, eleven airings were the number-one household-rated cable show for the day).

Once *HSM* hit the airwaves, weird things started happening everywhere. The first time the cast tried to go to the movies as a group on a Friday night after the premiere, they were instantly mobbed by fans. "We won't do that again," Vanessa told the *Los Angeles Daily News*.

Vanessa and Zac innocently tried to get together for a trip to the mall. But they were hounded by a bunch of fans who spotted them and instantly broke into singing the *HSM* songs. The two young actors watched incredulously as this crowd of kids started doing the dance moves from the movie while they belted out the lyrics! While shopping solo, Zac walked into a Tower Records and the room immediately went silent. Yikes! Totally freaked out, he hightailed it back to his car.

Everyone involved in *HSM* had high hopes, but nobody expected anything like this. The young stars were in shock at how quickly their little musical swept the nation. It was in magazines, on TV, in the newspaper. People couldn't get enough of it . . . or them. Zac was definitely not prepared for his newly found fame. "I'm sure I won't fully realize until I look back in five years and think, 'Oh, that was crazy,'" he told *TeenTelevision*.

Vanessa definitely found one big perk to fame. "Free stuff!" she told the *Plain Dealer*. "Clothes. An iPod. I got a new TV from Disney, which was very generous." In

fact, Disney gave each cast member of *HSM* a flat-screen. Come on, it's the least they could do.

Zac was just grateful that all this attention and fame could lead to more and better acting parts. "The most important thing is other opportunities to work, and working is really why we're doing all of this," he told the *Plain Dealer*. Nicely put, Zac (although he definitely liked the flat-screen as well).

No one, not even any of the bigwigs at Disney, can say for sure what made *HSM* the phenomenon it is. But its universal themes of being true-hearted, its cast of cute actors, and its great music all combined to create a rocket-fueled hit. "I knew we had something wonderful that everyone loved," Rich Ross, president of Disney Channel Worldwide, told the *Desert Morning News* in 2006. "I didn't realize when I said the word *everyone*, I meant everyone." Zac felt that the film was unique because parents and children could enjoy it together without feeling uncomfortable. The fantasy of musicals that drew him in as a kid now made millions happy. "There's something magical about

watching big production numbers," Zac told the *Edmonton Sun*, adding that girls "love the romance, and boys love the whole basketball and sports angle of the show."

The movie wasn't the only smash. Disney released the *HSM* album on January 10, a week and a half before the movie's premiere, and in only a few days, it was on fire. David Lawrence wrote the score, but five separate composing teams were assembled to write the songs. In total, there were about a dozen songwriters working to make the sound track. It really shows, since *HSM* has an eclectic mix of songs in a bunch of genres from hip-hop to pop to ballads. With all that, they recorded the entire album in an astounding five days.

Zac was no stranger to singing. He'd been belting out show tunes since he was a tiny kid. "I've always been singing. Since day one. I started doing musical theater and you have to sing in musical theater and so that's where I got most of my training," he told *Teen* magazine. Zac also took lessons, but that was all long ago. He admitted, "Slowly when you hit puberty, your voice sort of disappears in a weird way."

Despite whatever qualms Zac might have about his voice, he became the first artist to debut with two charted songs in the same week on the February 4, 2006, Billboard Hot 100! "Get'cha Head in the Game" and his duet with Vanessa, "Breaking Free," were the songs that put him in that historic position. "Breaking Free" had its own trajectory: The song made the fastest climb in the Billboard chart's history—going from number 86 to number 4 in just two weeks.

And that meant sales. Crazy sales. The *HSM* sound track went double platinum, with U.S. sales hitting 2.7 million albums! Twice it topped the Billboard charts, and for three weeks, it took the top spot on iTunes. During one week, it had nine singles on the charts at the same time. No one was more surprised than Zac. "When you go on the Billboard chart, you're looking at Mariah Carey, Kelly Clarkson, and *High School Musical*. No way!" he told *7M Pictures*. "They have a typo here." Even the National Basketball Association got into the act, using "Get'cha Head in the Game" for TV promotions.

Could *HSM* get any bigger? Um, yeah. That May, when the DVD went on sale, four hundred thousand copies flew out of the stores on the very first day! After it sold 1.2 million in the first six days, *HSM* became the fastest-selling television movie of all time. The DVD had two versions: one had a sing-along edition with on-screen lyrics. There were also added treats like a dance lesson by director Kenny Ortega and behind-the-scenes bloopers.

The DVD release on May 23 was such a big event, it got its own Hollywood premiere, with a red carpet, glamorous celebrities, a party, and everything! Not many DVDs can claim that. *American Idol's* Ace Young, *Dancing with the Stars's* Lisa Rinna, and Zac's *Summerland* buddy Lori Loughlin were among the many big names who joined the *HSM* cast to kick off the DVD. Vanessa looked hot strutting the red carpet in her Betsey Johnson sundress and wild makeup. Zac played it cool (just like a guy!) in a green T-shirt and jeans. Hundreds of screaming fans lined the red carpet leading up to El Capitan Theater, where the hit movie was screened. Then the young stars headed

over to the after-party at Hollywood & Highland—a thirty-thousand-square-foot, multi-level venue with restaurants and nightclubs—where they could joke around at the make-your-own video station featuring songs from the *HSM* sound track.

With DVDs and albums selling like hotcakes, *HSM* spawned a whole line of products. Disney released *HSM* "in a box," a set of materials that middle schools and high schools can use to produce their own versions of the musical. The president of the channel said they have already had forty thousand inquiries. There are *HSM* T-shirts, posters, and ringtones, and writers are hard at work on a novel!

The kids of *HSM* all embarked on a whirlwind of press tours, premieres, and promotions. Zac appeared on the *Jimmy Kimmel Show*, which he loved because he met one of his heroes, famed British actor Ian McKellen, who promised to give the young actor a tour of London whenever he came to town. Everyone in the cast was keeping busy. Ashley Tisdale quickly began working on an album, which she hopes to release in 2007. *Suite Life* fans don't have to

worry: She's keeping her day job as the lovable babysitter Maddie Fitzpatrick. Meanwhile, Vanessa Anne Hudgens is also working on a record deal. But for now, Corbin Bleu is sticking to acting with his new movie called *Jump* (his dad is also in the flick!).

HSM hasn't lost any steam, either. It earned a whopping six Emmy nominations for outstanding children's program, directing for a movie, casting for a movie, outstanding choreography, outstanding music, and outstanding lyrics.

If Zac found his new fame daunting, soon there'll be no place in the world for him to hide. In the summer of 2006, Disney started to air *HSM* in about a hundred countries. In most cases, the movie was simply dubbed into the country's language, but in India the music is being rerecorded in Hindi with top professional singers. Zac would be adorable no matter what language he's singing in!

chapter 9
Onward and Up

There's no doubt about it: Zac Efron is one of the biggest stars of his generation. He's not just breaking free—he's breaking records! According to the *San Luis Obispo Tribune*, in the month of January 2006, Zac was the second-highest-rising Google entertainment search subject. In that same month, IMDbPro's STARmeter ranked Zac as high as number four (that's out of *all* movie stars, from Johnny Depp to Hilary Duff!).

As a result of his superstar status, Zac's face is being splashed all over teen magazines, and there are countless fan sites devoted to him. For the most part, Zac enjoys the attention. "I love the discussions online," Zac confessed to *7M Pictures*. "They can pick out things in a movie that you'd never dreamed people would find out." Still, Zac is aware of the downside of living under the media microscope.

"I don't go online that often. I try not to because it can either give you a big head or tear you down."

Not surprisingly, you have a lot less privacy when you're a major celebrity. Some actors handle this fact better than others. Zac, for one, seems to be keeping his sense of humor. "I was at a Cheetah Girls concert a few weeks ago and a little girl came up and asked for an autograph," he told *Teen* magazine. "I said yes and pretty soon the whole audience wanted one. So many people came up that security had to escort me out of the building. They sort of threw me outside in the back alley and said I couldn't come in until the concert started. Pretty soon my good friend Ashley Tisdale was thrown out there, too."

Shopping is also a little bit harder than it used to be. "One time I got trapped in a mall with a friend and we had to run to leave the place," Zac recalled in *Lifetime* magazine. "I have to say that it's also completely different for me to have people go online to look at my pictures. And people sign on to have chats about me! It's so alien. It's really weird, because I'm just a regular person. It all gets

a little blown out of proportion. Not that I don't enjoy it, but it's just a weird feeling and kind of hard to describe."

But Zac seems willing to accept his responsibility as a role model. If that means reaching out to a crowd full of admiring fans, he'll do it. "Watching kids react is incredible," he said during a *PBS Kids* interview. "With kids you get a very pure sense of joy when they see you, and that's really fun. Because I remember when I was a kid—you used to see the people you look up to and when they sign that little piece of paper it made your day."

It's true—Zac used to be as obsessed over certain celebrities as his fans are over him. His dad remembers those days well. "We go to see the San Francisco Giants play one or two games per year," he told *J-14* magazine. "I have very fond memories of Zac waiting for hours for players to leave, hoping to get an autograph."

Although Zac is treated like a megastar by legions of fans, his lifestyle hasn't changed all that much. He's still pretty much the same old Zac. As he said to *PBS Kids*, "I don't have a fancy car. I don't live in a mansion. Everyone

thinks that along with the movie you get rewarded monetarily. You don't."

After graduating from high school with the class of 2006, Zac did move into a new home in North Hollywood, but it's a modest apartment, not a zillion-dollar estate with a swimming pool out back and a bowling alley in the basement (though that would be pretty sweet!).

There is one other thing that Zac decided to pay for, and that's having the tiny gap between his two front teeth closed. "My teeth got fixed by braces," he admitted to *BIG Star* magazine. "What happened was the gap was actually very small, and when I went on camera, especially on TV, it would just distort it and make it look really big. So first, we shrank it and then we closed it all the way. I think my teeth look a lot better." Some fans might argue that he looked cuter with the gap, but whatever makes Zac happy!

What really makes Zac the happiest is working. That's what he's been doing most often since making it big. Though despite what you might think, parts aren't

Zac and a friend in one of his first red-carpet appearances

Zac at a Disney Channel event wearing (what else?) his favorite necklace

Zac with his idol
Paula Abdul and a
friend at a WB event

Zac gettin'
down to his
hit song "We're
All in This
Together"

Laid-back Zac
chatting with fans

suddenly handed to you left and right once you're a star. "You know, everyone makes Hollywood out to be much more glamorous than it is," he told *Life Story* magazine. "You have no idea what the actors have to go through."

What they have to go through is endless auditions. There are probably ten times as many actors as there are available parts, so the competition is fierce, even for the A-list celebrities. "For every role that I have done on TV and movies, I've auditioned for thirty or forty," Zac told the *San Luis Obispo Tribune*. A lot of times, the casting agents will make it seem like he definitely got the part, only to turn around and give it to someone else. "It's ruthless. There are several thousand kids out there with brown hair and blue eyes that are my age trying to be in movies. Getting a job is like being in a casino." But as frustrated as Zac gets at times, he's not about to start compromising his integrity in any way just for the sake of a part. "I'm not going to be going out there having sex on-screen and stuff like that at this point in my career. I want to save a little of that young image that I've earned from the Disney Channel."

Plus, the fact of the matter is that Zac has been working steadily since the success of *High School Musical*. Some of the roles are large, some small. For instance, he played the main character in Hope Partlow's music video "Sick Inside" (Zac keeps his clothes on, of course, but it's still really steamy!).

Zac has also done a lot more work for television. He shot a pilot called *Heist*, about a gang of thieves who try to rob a bunch of jewelry stores in Beverly Hills during the week of the Academy Awards (when everyone in town is obviously a little distracted by other things!).

There's also the new show on Fox called *If You Lived Here, You'd Be Home by Now*, which is expected to be part of the fall 2006 lineup. It's a comedy about a group of people with different backgrounds who end up living in the same housing complex in Los Angeles. Zac plays the sixteen-year-old son of a single mother who is always struggling to make ends meet.

Probably the best television part Zac landed was a guest appearance on *The Suite Life of Zack & Cody*, the hit

Disney series starring the adorable Sprouse twins, Dylan and Cole. Zac was excited to work with the preteen celebs, but he was also psyched to be reunited with Ashley Tisdale, his costar from *High School Musical*. In the episode, called "Odd Couples," Zac plays a merit scholar named Trevor who is staying at the hotel where the show is set. Ashley's character and another girl both fall for the hunky Trevor, which kicks off a classic love triangle scenario.

Zac had a blast on the set, and he was really impressed by the Sprouses. "They're good kids," he told *Lifetime* magazine. "They're cool. They've got a lot of energy. They're amazing at what they do, and they're naturals. If I was their age, I would be so stressed out. I wouldn't know what was going on."

Filming the episode also gave Zac and Ashley a chance to talk about the most exciting news of the season: The executives at Disney had decided to make *High School Musical II*! No firm date for its release has been set, but there's been wide media speculation. It could be out in the winter of 2007—but it might be released earlier. Here's hoping!

There are a lot of rumors about the plot of *HSM II*, but it will almost definitely take place during East High's summer vacation. A lot of people think the action will occur at a country club that hosts an annual talent show. One thing is certain: The entire cast can't wait to get moving. Most of all Zac!

When *TeenTelevision* asked Zac if he'll try to play high-school students for as long as he can, he replied: "Yeah. I love it. I'm eighteen, but seriously, I'm operating on such a lower level. I'm young for my age. High school is a defining point in your history. Everyone remembers high school. At that age, there is so much drama and so many funny stories and great things happen. It shapes who you are. As long as we can portray this age group, I think I'm going to keep doing it."

As for what he's hoping for his character in the sequel, Zac told *TeenTelevision*, "I think there's not much more I can ask for. If Troy gets any cooler, he'll explode. I wish I was more like Troy. He can just keep on doing what he's doing." That may be true, but Zac did joke in the

Edmonton Sun that he wouldn't mind if it's revealed that "Troy is actually a secret agent or a superhero." That would really give him an advantage at the talent show!

Whatever happens, *HSM II* promises to be a sensation. But believe it or not, there's something just as big looming on the horizon for Zac. As much as he loves taking on teenage parts, Zac recently signed on to something that will definitely have him playing with the big boys.

chapter 10
Remaking a Masterpiece

E very generation has its hit movie musical. As crazy as audiences are today for *High School Musical*, in the eighties fans went almost as nuts for a little cult classic called *Hairspray*. The movie was written and directed by John Waters, who is known for his offbeat, often controversial style of filmmaking.

Set in the 1960s, the *Hairspray* story centers around a "pleasantly plump" teenager named Tracy Turnblad. She defies the odds and makes it as a regular dancer on the *Corny Collins Dance Show*, which airs in her hometown of Baltimore, Maryland. A power struggle ensues between Tracy and a rival dancer on the show called Amber von Tussle. Tracy not only wins the battle, she also wins the heart of hunky codancer Link Larkin. From there, the story

line takes a serious turn as Tracy uses her newfound fame to tackle the issue of racial inequality.

Considering what a huge hit the original *Hairspray* was, Zac definitely would have been intrigued when he heard about the remake. He no doubt read through all the casting calls that went out in 2006, but the part of Link Larkin must have really caught his eye. Here's how it read: *LINK. Male, Caucasian, 16–23 to play 17. Broadway quality Singer and Dancer. The teen heartthrob of 1962 Baltimore. Sexy. Hunky, with an edge (like a young Johnny Depp or Elvis). If you think you are our LINK, we want to see your taped audition immediately. HURRY! All materials MUST be received by Friday, May 19!*

Zac didn't waste any time sending off his taped audition. Unfortunately, neither did a few hundred other actors. At first, director Adam Shankman wasn't very interested in Zac, whose clean-cut image he found "very Disney, very Mouseketeery," as he told *Newsweek* in 2006. But Zac persisted, and in the end he was able to convince Shankman that he could bring a "little bit more

edge" to the dance. After a bunch of follow-up auditions, Shankman awarded Zac the part over two hundred other contenders!

Zac admitted to *Newsweek* that he's "pretty stoked" to be acting in *Hairspray*. That's sure playing it cool! After all, as successful as Zac has been in his career, this experience puts him in a whole new league. Just look at who some of his costars will be. Probably the biggest name is John Travolta, who, like Zac, had his breakout performance in a dance movie, the seventies sensation *Saturday Night Fever* (not to mention one of Zac's favorite musicals, *Grease*). Since then, Travolta has been in dozens of movies, earning millions and millions of dollars.

There's also Queen Latifah, the rapper-turned-movie-actress whose performance in the movie *Chicago* earned her an Oscar nomination. The list of topflight actors attached to the movie goes on and on, from Michelle Pfeiffer to Billy Crystal.

Some of the younger parts have gone to lesser-known stars, so Zac won't be totally intimidated by his

castmates (not that he would be, of course!). The lead role of Tracy Turnblad, for instance, will be played by seventeen-year-old Nicole Blonsky, whose only credits include plays she's acted in at South Senior High School in Great Neck, New York. Compared to that, Zac looks like a seasoned professional!

Whether A-list or unknown, the cast will be in good hands. The movie is being produced by Neil Meron and Craig Zadan. The talented duo was responsible for the making of *Chicago*, which won a total of six Academy Awards in 2002. Besides talent, they have a lot of money to play around with. The budget for *Hairspray* is expected to exceed fifty million dollars. (That's ten times the budget for *High School Musical*.)

Filming of *Hairspray* is set to start in fall 2006, and the movie will hopefully hit theaters in the spring of 2007. Though at one point, it was going to be shot in Baltimore, the producers decided to move it to Toronto. A lot of movies are made in this Canadian city because of its gigantic soundstages and relatively low production

costs. "When you do a big movie musical, you need huge soundstages because the sets are very big," producer Zadan explained to the *Associated Press* in 2006. "You also need a lot of ceiling space because you do a lot of sweeping crane shots, so you've got huge camera equipment."

Wow! This is all a far cry from the local community theater where Zac got his start acting almost eight years ago. Remember how he used to get excited about flying around the stage in a harness during performances of *Peter Pan*? Now he's got to get ready for sweeping crane shots! At this rate, it won't be long before Zac is making movies in a rocket ship high above the Earth's surface. But then, given how quickly his star has risen, somehow that doesn't seem all that impossible!

chapter 11
Just an Ordinary Superstar

Zac might be a superstar with a worldwide fan club, but beneath all the glamour and glitz of the red carpet, he's just a regular guy. Well, a regular hot guy. He's naturally a cutie, but he adds to the attraction by being totally health conscious—he stays away from drinking and smoking, and he would never, ever touch drugs. Zac is also a workout freak: He exercises all the time. "After watching the entire *Rocky* series, I got hooked on fitness," he told *Teen* magazine. But Zac insists he's no jock, especially not while he was in school. He certainly was no team captain. "All I played was Hacky Sack!" he told *Popstar!* magazine.

That's not totally true. Zac, with his adventurous attitude, will try just about any sport. When he was in junior high school, he got into skiing, golfing, rock climbing, and snowboarding. In sixth grade, his first big splurge was an

electric scooter, which he told *Teen* magazine "bankrupted me." All that zipping around was worth the financial strain. It didn't eclipse his skateboarding, though. He skateboarded everywhere when he was a kid, but once he started acting, it fell by the wayside.

One sport he picked up while acting is surfing. Catching waves became a passion after he spent long days on the beach shooting *Summerland*. The Christmas he was on the WB show he got a new board and wet suit as a gift. Zac must be amazingly gorgeous when he's all tousled from the sand and sea after a surfing session! He wasn't great at hanging ten right away. Once, he fell off his board and got crushed by a wave, which held him under the surf for ten seconds! "It was pretty scary," he told *Tiger Beat*. Not that it made him give up the sport. No way. "I'm hitting the waves all over the place," he told The WB.com. "We've had a couple of shark sightings, but so what. Here's the thing: If you get bit by a shark, you are the luckiest dude in the world because you are a legend forever."

If shark attacks aren't enough danger for our

favorite actor, skydiving is the next big thrill for Zac. He's dying to try that death-defying sport because he's always up for anything. Let's just hope he doesn't hurt himself on the way down!

Sports are only one way Zac shows he's still such a boy. Like most boys, he finds it really funny being gross. "I can blow spit bubbles with my tongue after I eat a Starburst," he told *J-14* magazine. "I've actually changed lives." Yuck!

Spit bubbles aside, Zac isn't above doing anything to get a laugh. One year, he went to camp and everyone was doing skits around a bonfire. It was a competition, and to get an award, the boys had to come up with something special. "My dorm decided to dress me up in women's clothing, and I had to get up onstage!" he told *Popstar!* magazine. They didn't put him in a dress, but he wore long gloves and other ladylike things. Then his campmates sang "My Little Lollipop" around him. Not exactly *High School Musical* caliber entertainment. "It was so embarrassing, but we won!"

On the more macho end of things, Zac loves to watch anything on Spike, a cable network geared toward guys. And he loves going to San Francisco Giants games with his dad whenever he can get away. But he's a big baby when it comes to horror movies. He can't take them because "lately they've been so scary!" he told *Tiger Beat*. Awww! Comedies are more his speed. Zac takes any opportunity he can to pop in his well-watched copy of *Goonies* and laugh his head off at the goofy kids' flick.

And he's not too old for baseballs, either. Zac says his autographed baseball collection is his most prized possession, and with all the money he's made from *HSM*, he must have a lot of great stuff. He told *Teen* magazine, "I've got almost every player from the Giants for the past ten years—except Barry Bonds. I'm working on that." That'd be the perfect birthday gift for the guy who has everything.

Right now, Zac has a new obsession—fixing up old cars. His hobby started when his grandfather gave him three cars! And not some old grampa-mobiles. These wheels are the slickest, even in California, where the competition is hot

for cool cars. He's working on an orange-red '65 Mustang convertible and a late '90s Oldsmobile Alero. The Mustang is really rare because "in '64 they barely made any, so we have the first real year!" Zac explained to *Popstar!* magazine. But his hot rod is far from ready to hit the road. "I think my grandpa caught the engine on fire, but we're trying to get it started anyway!"

He's also tinkering with a silver DeLorean. "It's the car from *Back to the Future*," he told *J-14* magazine. "As soon as I can get a time-flux capacitor, I'm set." That's a lot of tough car talk, but in reality, his dad is the main mechanic. "I sort of just hand him the wrench; that's my position," he told *Popstar!* magazine. "I'm like the tool go-getter! He takes care of most of the work."

Between the cars and the extreme sports, you'd think Zac didn't have a softer side. But he does. First off, he is into clothes and cares about looking good. His favorite article of clothing is his Gucci aviators, which he called the "best present ever."

He's also attached to another present, a star

necklace he wears a lot. So who's the special lady who gave it to him? "It's actually from Paula Abdul's line," he told *TeenTelevision*. The *American Idol* judge put it on him, and he hasn't taken it off since. The star says, *Reach for the stars!* That's a pretty good gift from one star to another.

One of Zac's favorite ways to kick back is with a good book (he also has a major comic book collection). "In a few pages of a book, you can find ten times as much detail as a movie or a TV show," he told *Life Story*. Not that he has any problems with movies and television. "I love movies and TV. I think they're equally educational."

With his busy acting schedule and all his hobbies, it's amazing, but Zac has found the time to teach himself to play the guitar. He has a musical background. He took piano lessons for a few years. But like a lot of kids, he quit. Still, he took with him a few musical skills—including the ability to sight-read music. He's putting those lessons toward the guitar now. To speed along his learning, Gibson gave him a free guitar, which he's been playing nonstop. He told *Teen* magazine, "I'm starting to hopefully write songs." We hope so, too, Zac!

chapter 12
Life as Usual

So what's an ordinary day like in the life of Zac Efron? There are some things that might shock you.

Well, first off, Zac's not exactly a morning person. In fact, early morning is kind of a blur for him. "I wake up somehow—I don't know if I'm on all fours, but somehow I make it to the shower and then I wake up in there!" he told *Popstar!* magazine. Once under the water, though, this sleepy cutie comes alive. Zac starts his day by belting out songs—but not onstage. These tunes are in the shower because he loves to sing while soaping up.

Zac says a perfect day begins with a nice long run. It all goes into his complete routine to combat the stress of being one of today's hottest young stars. "I eat right, exercise, and sleep a lot!" he told *PBS Kids*.

We know Zac is crazy for cereal, but he can't exist

on that alone. What's his idea of eating "right"? Well, Zac may be a lot of things—good friend, good actor, good-looking—but he's no cook. He eats sushi and anything else that he can order in a restaurant. But whenever he has to fend for himself for dinner, he resorts to the easiest recipe in the book: mac and cheese. "All the other stuff is too hard!" he told *Teen* magazine.

Zac's lack of culinary skill is a major obstacle now that he has his own apartment in LA. Since his career's taken off, Zac needed an apartment closer to auditions. So now he lives in that cool apartment in North Hollywood. He's tried to make it cozy: There's a loft bed with a couch and a recliner chair underneath where he likes to watch TV or dive into a book. That's when he can tear himself away from his two favorite gadgets—his iPod and mobile phone.

And if he's a bad cook, he's a worse maid. Zac definitely has a problem cleaning up. Really, Zac is a major slob. "There are dirty clothes everywhere," he told *J-14* magazine.

Sounds like the Hollywood apartment is 100

percent Zac. But that doesn't mean he thinks of it as home. No, home is still Arroyo Grande, at his parents' house. Moving out of his childhood home has been tough on Zac. "It's different. I'm not living in the San Luis Obispo area anymore," he told *J-14* magazine. "I've lived there my whole life. It's a transition, but it makes going home so much fun."

A lot of kids would kill to have their own apartment. But our sensitive Zac finds any reason he can to go home. And when he can't go back to Arroyo Grande, Zac calls his dad at night to share the ups and downs of his day. His parents, Starla and Dave, want him to branch out on his own. They're trying to help him become more independent so that he doesn't have to come home so much. It's pretty cute, though, that he gets so homesick!

Zac's not letting go so easily. "Being with my family these days is a treat," Zac told *J-14* magazine. "You have to remember as you grow up that friends will always stick by you, but your family even more so. Your family will always be inside your heart and by your side—no matter what."

Who can argue with that?

When he's back in Arroyo Grande, Zac loves playing with his pets, two Australian shepherds called Dreamer and Puppy, and a Siamese cat named Simon. "My dogs are crazy. They're always getting into some kind of trouble . . . but then again, they're my most loyal friends," he told zefron.com. He's so devoted to his pooches that when he's home, Zac wakes up at 6:30 A.M. to take the dogs out for a run even before the sun is up! Dreamer was his first pet, but in later years, she got really fat and had trouble running. "We put her on a diet," Zac told *Popstar!* magazine. Hey, just like a Hollywood star. "Now she's back to normal. She can actually run, so we're having fun. I'm trying to teach her to catch a Frisbee, but it doesn't seem to always work."

Despite his parents' wish for him to become independent, it seems like they miss him just as much as he does them. In Arroyo Grande, it's still like Zac Efron central. On the kitchen table, there are stacks and stacks of *HSM* movie posters, teen magazines, and newspaper clippings Zac's dad has collected. There are also scripts

Zac's considering and has brought home to read. According to *Teen* magazine, the young actor sums up this house as "where my heart is."

When Zac gets down from all the stress and strain of auditions, he doesn't just rely on his folks or the cozy confines of his childhood bedroom and backyard. He has another source to turn to: his best friends.

His main posse is made up of seven boys—Taylor, Shane, Connor, Chris, Bubba, Bryce, and Jorn—all guys he's known forever. "I've hung out with them all the way from diapers to this day," he told *Bop* magazine.

Zac's pals haven't been changed by his success. Well, at least his real friends, the core group he's hung out with ever since he can remember. Those who are jealous don't remain in his inner circle. In fact, he's the only one in his group who acts and sings. "I'm lucky enough to have friends that are so far removed from the industry that they do not care," he told *7M Pictures*. "I come home and it's a reality check."

They are a diverse group of guys. One of them is

going to be a professional basketball player. Another is headed to college to study computers. It's a real spectrum. "We're all very different, but opposites attract," he told *Bop*. "I never really had to look for friends because I always knew I had my buddies back home."

Just because they aren't in show business doesn't mean his friends don't have an opinion on his acting. Zac encourages them to express their thoughts on his projects. He's grateful for their comments because he knows they're real. "The best advice they give me is to critique my work," he told *Bop*. "It brings us all back down to earth."

When they get together, it's not earth-shattering stuff. No paparazzi or groupies. They just hang out and play cards like normal friends.

Zac doesn't see his pals from his hometown as often as he'd like, but when they hang out, it's like no time has passed or hit movies have been made. "I wish I had more spare time [to] hang out with [my] friends, goof off, be a kid," he told *PBS Kids*. "It can be a little tough to see my friends because I'm gone so much, but I'm enjoying it."

Text messaging helps a lot. Zac's practically physically attached to his phone. "One month I had around fifteen hundred text messages with friends," he told *Tiger Beat*. Wow! Luckily, he can afford the bill. And it's worth the sky-high cell phone statement. "It's just great to know that no matter what happens, I have my friends at home," he told *Bop*. "They are my comfort factor."

But what about girls? Is there anyone special who's part of Zac's comfort factor?

chapter 13
Love Life

Zac's characters go by different names, but they all have a bit of the Casanova in them, from Cameron Bale to Troy Bolton to Link Larkin. But what about in real life? Is Zac as interested in the opposite sex as the hopeless romantics he plays on film and television? You bet he is!

From the sound of it, Zac has always had a way with the ladies, even back in elementary school. "I was in first grade, and this girl passed me a note in the middle of class that said, 'Do you like me?' and there was a box that said, 'Check yes or check no.' I checked yes and handed it back to her. It was really funny, romantic awesomeness."

Despite his early start, it would be many years before Zac experienced his first kiss—seven, to be exact, though beyond that, the details are a little sketchy. "I was in the eighth grade and it was with a girl named . . . shoot!"

Zac said in an interview with *Popstar!* magazine, forgetting the name of the lucky gal. "I can picture her face exactly! I can't believe I can't think of her name!" Zac never did remember the name, but he did recall that the big moment occurred during a game of truth or dare.

Game playing aside, Zac actually takes dating pretty seriously. For one thing, he's not the type to love 'em and leave 'em. "My first crush and I are still friends to this day," he told *Tiger Beat* magazine in 2006. "We text message and call each other all the time."

Zac has also put a lot of thought into the kind of girl he wants to be with. He's not the type to go out with anyone just for the sake of having another date. So what is his type? "I love it when girls have self-confidence," he admitted to *Tiger Beat* magazine. "If you can forget you're talking, and you look at your watch and see you've just spent two hours chatting, then that's when you know you've found someone that you could be with."

Apparently, it also doesn't hurt if the girl smells really nice! When *J-14* magazine asked Zac what makes for

a really great kiss, he replied: "A good perfume. I like the smell of Pink Sugar." Got that, girls?

As for turnoffs, Zac is definitely into healthy gals, telling *People* magazine that he wouldn't even consider going out with a smoker. He also likes a girl who can focus on the conversation and not some song in her head. "If you're on a date, don't be constantly humming a song," he told *PBS Kids*. "I was with a person who was doing that and it was *so* annoying!"

Pet peeves aside, Zac's approach to dating is a lot like his approach to acting. Basically, his motto is that you can't be afraid or you'll never get anywhere. "Ask out your crushes!" Zac proclaimed in *Popstar!* magazine. "And when you do, you'll be so happy you did it! You gotta put yourself out there, because if you do, you'll have no regrets!"

Still, even Zac admits that he sometimes gets nervous before asking someone out. "It can be so hard," he said during an interview with *Bop* magazine. "The thing that's always going through my mind is, 'Does she like me at all?'" In those moments, Zac likes to play it cool. "I'll start up a

conversation and not lead on at all that I like them. I get them talking and if they talk back, and we eventually find a connection, that's good, and if we don't, it's over."

One thing Zac doesn't do is hem and haw. "The worst thing to do is stew on the perfect way to approach a girl," he said during the same *Bop* magazine interview. "If you do that, then you think about it too much and you're bound to mess it up. If you just go out there and start giving hints and being yourself around the girl, hopefully she returns some of the vibe and you guys click. . . . Just go with your gut and be yourself."

Of course, Zac does admit that being a megastar makes it a little bit easier to meet tons of good-looking, talented people. "Yeah! That was one of the benefits of being in [*High School Musical*]," he told *Teen Television*. "Lots of pretty girls. I don't think there were necessarily any on-set romances. But we immediately all became fast friends."

Even if the cast members of *High School Musical* were just friends, rumors started to swirl around the set

right away. Zac was almost always at the center of them! Some involved an alleged romance with his costar Vanessa Anne Hudgens, while others had him being more than just friends with Ashley Tisdale. But all three actors insist the reports were nothing more than rumors that had taken on a life of their own.

"Ashley is one of my best friends, and we're really cool," Zac told *J-14* magazine. "But I don't think we're going to be dating anytime soon. I think we're close in other ways. However, there's really no telling what the future holds." As for Vanessa, Zac admits to being very fond of her as well, but "not in a loving way. We hang out together. She loves shopping, so we go to the mall."

The rumors about Zac and Ashley didn't die down any when he made a guest appearance on *The Suite Life of Zack & Cody*. The fact that a lot of sparks flew between their characters in the episode only added to the gossip. The show's writers had a lot to do with that, sneaking a surprise kiss into the episode at the last minute. "[Zac] came in on the day we were going to rehearse and sees

this scene that was just rewritten," Ashley told *Popstar!* magazine. "It was a total surprise for all of us. It was not in the episode at first!" Apparently, it took five takes before Zac figured out how to properly lock lips with Ashley. "Zac likes to do 'WB kissing' and that was not Disney-esque!" the actress explains, referring to Zac's steamy make-out scenes with Kay Panabaker on *Summerland*. "They said, 'Zac, you've got to calm down, okay?' " Not that Ashley was complaining. "It was good," she admits. "He's a good kisser!"

But even after the on-screen kiss, Zac and Ashley still denied any rumors of romance. "I think it's just funny," Zac told *Twist* magazine in 2006. "Me and Ashley are good friends. We just laugh every time we hear it! She's very cool and we hang out all the time, but we're definitely not dating."

So if not Ashley or Vanessa or any of the other beautiful actresses he comes in contact with, then who is Zac dating? For the moment, the answer is no one, but as he said to *News for Kids*, "I'm working on it." Though

he's admitted numerous times that his dream lady is Jessica Alba, it's more likely that he hasn't yet met the perfect someone. He is even open to the possibility of love at first sight. "Sure, it's a complete reality," he told *Tiger Beat* magazine. "I think that would be a great way to fall in love! I mean, how can you go wrong with that!"

But just as Zac has never forced his acting career, only focusing on the roles that are best suited for him, he's not about to rush headlong into love. As he explained to *J-14* magazine, "I like to think I haven't been in love yet because I want that to be special." One thing is certain: Zac is going to make some lucky lady out there very happy someday—hopefully soon!

chapter 14
Looking Ahead

Zac's future is wide open. Still a teen, he's got a rockin' career going that looks to have a long future ahead. But through all the hard work it took for him to achieve stardom, Zac never let his grades go by the wayside. Throughout high school, he successfully managed his acting career and schoolwork. When he couldn't go to public school because of his busy schedule, he had a tutor. Whatever the setting, he maintained a 4.3 grade-point average and graduated in the summer of 2006. "My priority had always been school first, acting second," he told *Scholastic News*. "I have a really high grade-point average, but if I hadn't taken the acting route, I think I might have been valedictorian."

He applied to two colleges, the University of

Southern California and the University of California, Los Angeles—both California state schools. USC has a great film program while UCLA is great for musical theater, so either would work for Zac. Surprise, surprise—he got into both schools. In the end, film won out and Zac chose USC. However, because his career is white-hot right now, he's delayed enrolling.

Although he's holding off on college for the near future, Zac doesn't have any plans to leave his home state. "I definitely want to stay in California," he told *Popstar!* magazine. "I went to New York and had an amazing time, but I couldn't live there. It's too fast-paced. California's much more laid-back. I'm just a California boy."

His dad is super-pleased with all his son's accomplishments. "I'm proud of his approach to acting, remaining grounded despite his success, excelling academically, and being accepted to UCLA [and USC]," Dave told *J-14* magazine. "It's [a] good feeling to be referred to as Zac's dad."

Dave Efron might be over the moon about his

son's career, but Zac is taking everything in stride. After *High School Musical*, everyone was chasing after Zac to get him to make an album. He had all those hits on Billboard and he plays piano and guitar. The idea was obvious. But Zac decided to concentrate on one thing at a time and hold off on the whole music idea. "I like to sing, but I'm not looking for a record label or anything," he told zefron.com.

If he did, he wouldn't want a team of songwriters and musicians to whip up a phony album for him. "I would really put my heart and soul into an album," he told *Teen* magazine. "I would sit down with a guitar and write eleven or twelve good songs for an album, and that is gonna take a long time." Don't hold your breath for Zac's album. He's focusing on acting for the time being. He wants to build a true and solid foundation for his career. "The most important thing is to establish myself as an actor," he told *TeenTelevision*.

In terms of future film projects, Zac dreams about working with the best actors in the business. Two actresses

on the top of his list are Reese Witherspoon and Catherine Zeta-Jones. Whether that's for their acting talents or their beauty, he'll never tell.

But Zac does have another secret passion: directing. "As much as it's a performing art, I'm not really a performer," he told *TeenTelevision*. "I want to be behind the camera." Zac, not a performer? Wow, he fooled half the universe with that one. Zac fans, don't worry that he's throwing in the towel on his acting career anytime soon. "I would like to make my mark in front of the camera first before I endeavor to get behind it." Phew!

In fact, when asked by *PBS Kids* where he saw himself in ten years, Zac said, "I'd like to see myself still doing this. *High School Musical Number 48*." Amen to that!

chapter 15
Fun, Fast Facts

Are you Zac's biggest fan? Is your room papered with pictures of the *High School Musical* cutie? Can you sing every lyric from his *HSM* songs? Well, test your knowledge of all things Zac and see how many of the following facts you already know.

1. Name: Zachary David Alexander Efron
2. Birth date: Sunday, October 18, 1987
3. Birthplace: San Luis Obispo, California
4. Current home: Hollywood
5. Zodiac sign: Libra
6. Parents: David and Starla
7. Siblings: Dylan
8. Pets: Two Australian shepherds, Dreamer and Puppy, and a Siamese cat, Simon
9. Favorite cartoon: *Rocco's Modern Life*

10 Most prized possession: His autographed baseball collection

11. Favorite book: *Robinson Crusoe,* by Daniel Defoe

12. Favorite movie: *Goonies* and *Dumb and Dumber*

13. Dream role: Spider-Man

14. Favorite TV show: *Most Extreme Elimination* and *That '70s Show*

15. Favorite fast-food snack: Honey mustard chicken sandwich with bacon from Quiznos. "You know heaven?" Zac said. "It's kinda like that!"

16. Celebrity whose autograph Zac most wants: Los Angeles Lakers guard Kobe Bryant

17. Dream car: Toyota Supra from *The Fast and the Furious*

18. Zac has prescription contact lenses but never wears them.

chapter 16
Zac's Discography

Even before Zac was talking in complete sentences, he was humming along to his favorite tunes. As he got older, listening to music definitely evolved into one of his favorite hobbies. Though he's talked about maybe someday pursuing a career in music (especially after hanging out with rocker Jesse McCartney on the set of *Summerland*), for the moment, he's just a fan. But he's a *huge* fan. In fact, whether he's filming a movie or just kicking back at home, Zac is never far from his iPod. Though he's probably downloaded thousands of songs, here's a sampling of the musicians and sound tracks that Zac considers his current favorites.

Jack Johnson

This Hawaii-born singer and songwriter used to be a professional surfer, so it's no wonder Zac's a fan! Johnson was in a pretty bad surfing accident a while back, and it was during his recovery that he started penning songs and playing the guitar. His music is totally laid-back and mellow, the kind of stuff that's perfect to listen to on the beach as the sun's going down—which Zac no doubt does all the time! Johnson's 2003 album, *On and On*, debuted at number three on the Billboard 200 on the strength of its hit single "The Horizon Has Been Defeated." Check it out!

Ben Harper

Harper's music is also super-chill. The California native actually took Jack Johnson under his wing at one time, so it's no wonder they have similar sounds and that Zac digs them both equally. As his latest album, *Both Sides of the Gun*, proves, Harper is a little more versatile than Johnson. Sometimes he's folksy, sometimes he's bluesy, and sometimes he rocks it out. But as far as Zac is concerned, he's always totally awesome!

John Mayer

This twenty-eight-year-old singer-songwriter is probably best known for his song "Your Body Is a Wonderland," from

the album *Room for Squares*. The catchy single won him the Grammy Award for Best Male Pop Vocal Performance in 2003. He's another artist known for soulful lyrics and soft, melodious guitar playing. Mayer's tunes are usually really romantic—perfect "date music," as Zac has no doubt discovered!

The Shins

This band consists of four guys from Albuquerque, New Mexico, though they now call Portland, Oregon, home. Their sound is usually described as "indie rock." It's inspired by many different music genres, including pop, alternative, folk, and even country. Two tracks from The Shins' album *Oh, Inverted World* are on the sound track to the movie *Garden State* (which is another one of Zac's favorites). The track "Know Your Onion!" was used on an episode of *Gilmore Girls*, and the band even appeared on the show!

Avenue Q Sound Track

By far, the tunes that are getting the most play from Zac are those featured on the sound track to the hit Broadway musical *Avenue Q*. "Like the top twenty-five most-played songs on my iPod are from that play!" he told *Popstar!* magazine. The musical tells the story of a recent Princeton

grad who comes to New York City to make it big (Avenue Q is the name of the neighborhood where he ends up living). It features one hit song-and-dance routine after another—and Zac loves them all!

The Postal Service

While *Avenue Q* keeps Zac happy, when his spirits are low, he turns to another album. "When I'm down, I listen to The Postal Service," he admitted to *Tiger Beat* magazine. The band's name, in case you're curious, refers to the way its members would trade tapes and music by mail. The music definitely couldn't be described as happy, with its gut-wrenching lyrics and brooding melodies. But even Zac has his down moments, and it's the perfect music to go along with them.

Coldplay

Zac is really into international music, including this alternative rock band from London, England. They're pretty well-known in the United States, in part because their lead singer, Chris Martin, is married to famous actress Gwyneth Paltrow. Coldplay songs contain the introspective lyrics that Zac obviously looks for in a band. It's no wonder Coldplay features prominently on his personal playlist.

Matt Costa

This is one of Zac's more recent discoveries. Matt was initially a skateboarder, but an awful accident ended his career. Just as Jack Johnson did after he hurt himself surfing, Matt started making music while he was recovering from his injury. At first, he only shared the results with close friends in his California hometown. But the songs were so good that his reputation quickly spread. Always in the know, Zac was quick to hear about the up-and-coming star, and he's been listening ever since.

Hairspray Sound Track

Listening to the original sound track from this movie musical is part pleasure, part work, since Zac is all set to play the part of Link Larkin in the upcoming remake. Zac always researches his roles thoroughly, so he definitely has every lyric from every tune memorized by now. It's going to be awesome to hear his own renditions of the songs!

chapter 17
Online Sightings

Zac is full of energy and on the go in every way. In only a few years, his life has changed radically from that of a young kid doing regional musical theater to that of an international celebrity. His whirlwind style doesn't show any signs of petering out. So if you want to catch up on the latest news about Zac, check out the sites listed below. You should always get a parent's permission before signing online, and keep in mind that websites are always coming and going!

Official Zac Efron website:

www.zefron.com

Zac Efron picture gallery:

zac-efron-picture.blogspot.com

Internet Movie Database:

www.imdb.com/name/nm1374980

The Zac Efron forum on the official Disney Channel:

disneychannelforum.jconserv.net

High School Musical fan site:

**www.freewebs.com/
highschoolmusicalfanforlife8907**

High School Musical site:

www.disneychannel.com